Specifically tors interested business, this important and invaluable book provides a concise guide to understanding accountants' statements and their use in management.

"Professor Myer has developed a unique course in which he provides the necessary knowledge of the form, content, nature and use of the financial statements and the accounting processes . . . without requiring the student to learn laborious techniques of keeping the accounting records . . . should serve as a most useful source for all managerial personnel."

—From the Foreword by
Dr. Denis Sinclair Philipps.
Director of General Education
and Extension Services,
New York University

JOHN N. MYER is the author of *Accounting for Non-Accountants, Financial Statement Analysis and What the Investor Should Know About Corporate Financial Statements*. A teacher for over thirty years, he is a frequent contributor to business periodicals and a consultant to industry on executive training.

All About Business from the MENTOR Library

UNDERSTANDING FINANCIAL STATEMENTS

originally titled: *What the Executive Should Know about the Accountant's Statements*

John N. Myer

**The Management Institute
Division of General Education
and Extension Services
New York University**

A MENTOR BOOK
NEW AMERICAN LIBRARY

NEW YORK AND SCARBOROUGH, ONTARIO

MENTOR TRADEMARK REG. U.S. PAT. OFF. AND FOREIGN COUNTRIES
REGISTERED TRADEMARK—MARCA REGISTRADA
HECHO EN WINNIPEG, CANADA

SIGNET, SIGNET CLASSIC, MENTOR, PLUME, MERIDIAN AND NAL
BOOKS are published *in the United States* by
New American Library,
1633 Broadway, New York, New York 10019,
in Canada by The New American Library of Canada Limited,
81 Mack Avenue, Scarborough, Ontario M1L 1M8

FIRST MENTOR PRINTING, JANUARY, 1968

10   11   12   13   14   15   16   17   18

PRINTED IN CANADA

Foreword

IT HAS BEEN made evident that many of those who are taking courses in The Management Institute and attending the workshop seminars in various areas of management have experienced a disadvantage from not having an adequate understanding of how to interpret and use the data contained in the income statements, retained earnings statements, balance sheets, and other statements prepared by accountants. Although these students may at one time have studied accounting they usually have not received adequate instruction with respect to the use of the statements as an integral part of the management process.

Still others enrolled in The Management Institute, especially those participating in its Executive Management Program—professional engineers, physicists, or those engaged in other forms of applied science—have found themselves placed in a senior management position in which they are required to make decisions based on accounting statements. Not anticipating the need for a knowledge of accounting, they received no formal training in the subject. At this point in their professional careers it is hardly practical or desirable to recommend an introductory course in accounting and then a course in financial statement analysis. Even the reading of selected chapters from standard texts has not proved satisfactory in meeting the special needs of these students.

I am happy to report that to meet the needs of both of the categories of professional men and women described above, Professor Myer has developed a unique course in which he provides the necessary knowledge of the form, content, nature, and use of the financial statements. In addition he provides an understanding of the accounting processes, of which the financial statements are the result, without requiring the student to learn the laborious technique of keeping the accounting records. For this course the present book has been prepared as the text. On the basis of our experience in The Management Institute the text should serve in its own right as a most useful source for all managerial personnel who find themselves confronted with the need for the special kind of knowledge relating to the use and interpretation of the statements mentioned above.

DENIS SINCLAIR PHILIPPS, Ph.D.
Director, The Management Institute
Division of General Education and
    Extension Services
New York University

Preface

A FEW YEARS AGO I said it could not be done; that is, the explanation of the use of the accountant's statements to those who had not studied the technique of accounting. To such persons my statement seemed unreasonable. For to them the balance sheet appeared to be simply a list of what a business owns and what it owes, the difference being what it is worth. And the income statement appeared to be a report on the income of a business from which were deducted the expenses to arrive at the net income.

These popular notions are but misleading oversimplifications. At best they are only half-truths because, while the balance sheet purports to measure the assets, the liabilities, and the capital, and the income statement the revenue, the expenses, and the net income, the nature of the items contained in the statements is such that they cannot be measured easily or precisely. Added to this is the fact that the unit of measurement—the dollar—is an unstable one. How the accountant treats the problem is learned in the study of the technique of accounting. So that those who have been instructed in this technique should be able to understand the data contained in the final product of the accounting processes, the financial statements.

Now, as time passed and pressure by those desiring to learn about the use of the accountant's statements was mounting, I sought ways and means of imparting to these persons an understanding of the data contained in the statements without subjecting them to the process of studying the mechanics of accounting. The present book is the result.

After having been provided with an adequate knowledge of the nature of the data contained in the statements, the reader is given instruction in the use of these data for the purpose of forming an opinion concerning the condition of a business and for making managerial decisions.

For those desiring to enlarge their understanding of the subject, there is available a work book containing problems to be solved and questions to be answered. Solutions and answers are also contained in the work book.

JOHN N. MYER

September, 1964

Contents

Contents

UNDERSTANDING
FINANCIAL
STATEMENTS

1. Financial Position

THE FINANCIAL POSITION of a business is determined from a review of its assets, its liabilities, and its capital.

ASSETS

The *assets* of a business are the things owned by it. But in order to be an asset within the scope of accounting a thing must have the quality of being measurable in terms of money. For example, although a supply of fresh air in an office is very important to those who work there, the accountant does not regard fresh air as an asset. It is what the economist calls a "free good." You cannot say that it is worth a specific number of dollars. It might be said that to the accountant "if it cannot be measured in terms of money, it is not an asset." The monetary unit, in the United States the dollar, is thus the common denominator of accounting.

The assets of a business comprise not only cash and such property as land, buildings, machinery, furniture and fixtures, merchandise, and so forth, but also investments in securities and claims for sums of money owed to it by individuals or other businesses, known as *receivables*.

CAPITAL

Where do the assets come from? They are put into the business either by the owner or owners, in a corporation the stockholders, or they are put in by others. The total of that

13

portion of the assets put in by the owners, stated in terms of money, is called their investment or *capital*. This word has thus been given a meaning in accounting different from its meaning in economics, where it is used to denote the property or "wealth" owned by a business.

Assets come into a business not only by direct contribution but also as a result of earnings through the operation of the business. The increase in assets by earnings is in the nature of contribution by the owners and so increases the capital. Thus capital may be increased not only through investment by the owners but also by the earning of *income*, or *revenue*.

In contrast to the increase in capital through the earning of income, there is usually also a decrease in capital as the result of *expenses* incurred in order to earn the income. Salaries, rent, taxes, interest on indebtedness, and the cost of various services are examples of expenses. There are, accordingly, two forces constantly at work that affect the capital: income which increases it, and expenses which decrease it.

LIABILITIES

When assets are contributed to a business not as a capital investment, those who contribute them are known as creditors of the business. Contribution by creditors takes place when the asset cash is loaned to the business or when merchandise or other assets are sold to it but payment therefor is to be made at some future time. Creditors who have sold property to the business expect to receive from it a specific sum of cash at a certain date, in accordance with the terms of sale.

From the time money is loaned or goods are sold to a business until the date of payment the creditors are contributors to the assets possessed by it. Creditors, therefore, have an interest in the business and may be considered temporary investors.

When expenses are not paid for at the time they are incurred but are to be paid for at some future time, their amounts are recorded as *liabilities* and these are referred to as *payables*. Thus liabilities may increase not only as the result of contributions of assets by creditors but also through the incurring of expenses.

THE ACCOUNTING EQUATION

Since there are two sources from which the assets of a business are derived—creditors and owners—it follows that at any particular time the total of the assets will be equal to the total of the contributions of the creditors and the owners. This fact may be expressed in the form of an equation:

$$\text{ASSETS} = \text{LIABILITIES} + \text{CAPITAL}$$

The contributions of the creditors and owners are referred to as their interests or *equities* in the assets.

To use a simple illustration, if a certain business has assets amounting to $15,000 and $6,000 of these were acquired on credit, the capital is $9,000. Substituting these figures in the above equation, we have:

$$\$15,000 = \$6,000 + \$9,000$$

This relationship of assets, liabilities, and capital is a self-evident truth or axiom.

CLASSIFICATION OF ASSETS AND LIABILITIES

Some assets are of a relatively permanent nature; it is necessary for the business to have them in order to carry on its activities. Examples of such assets are: a building, furniture and fixtures, and automobiles. These assets the accountant classifies as *fixed assets*.

In contrast to these, there are other assets that are continually moving into and out of the business, or are being converted from one form to another. Examples of such assets are: cash, receivables, either in the form of promissory notes or "charge accounts," and an inventory or stock of goods for sale. These assets the accountant classifies as *current assets*.

The accountant also classifies the liabilities into two general groups. The grouping is made with regard to the time when the liability must be paid. If the liability is to

be paid within a year, it is classified as a *current liability*;
if due within more than one year, it is placed in the cate-
gory of a *long-term liability*. Of course, as the maturity of a
long-term liability approaches to within a year, it becomes
a current liability.

Examples of current liabilities are: notes payable and
accounts payable, depending on whether they are represented by promissory notes or "charge accounts," if due
within a year, which is usually the case in ordinary business transactions. An example of a long-term liability is a
mortgage on a building maturing in more than one year.

2. The Financial Statements

AT THE END of a period of time, usually a year, the accountant prepares for a business certain statements that present the results of the accounting for that period. These statements comprise: (1) the balance sheet or statement of financial position, (2) the profit and loss statement or income statement, and, in the case of corporations, (3) the surplus statement or retained earnings statement. These statements, taken together, are usually referred to as *the financial statements*.

The reader may well wonder why each statement has alternative titles. The reason is that one is an older and the other is a newer title. The first title here given for each statement is the older one. There are others in use but those given are the titles commonly employed. In the interest of simplicity, the titles usually used throughout this book will be those in most common use at the present time: the balance sheet, the income statement, and the retained earnings statement.

THE BALANCE SHEET

The balance sheet shows the financial position of a business as of the close of business on a certain date by presenting a review of its assets, its liabilities, and its capital. The financial position is traditionally reviewed at the end of each accounting period. Obviously, the financial position as of the close of business on the last day of a period will be the same at the commencement of business on the first day of the following period.

THE INCOME STATEMENT

The income statement contains a summary, for a certain period, of the income of a business and the expenses incurred in earning that income. The expenses are deducted from the income to obtain the difference called the *net income* or *net loss* for the period—net income if the income is the greater and net loss if the expenses are the greater.

THE RETAINED EARNINGS STATEMENT

The retained earnings statement (used in the case of corporations) shows the amount of accumulated earnings at the beginning of a period not distributed to stockholders, the amount of net income for the period added thereto, or net loss deducted therefrom, the amount paid out to the stockholders deducted, and other additions to and deductions from the accumulated earnings. It concludes with the amount of undistributed earnings at the end of the period.

SOURCE OF THE FINANCIAL STATEMENT DATA

The data contained in the financial statement are obtained from the accounting records. Since it is not within the scope of this book to explain these records or how the accounting data are processed therein,* it will suffice here to say that the records from which the data contained in the financial statements are obtained are called *accounts*.

The balance sheet comprises a showing of the amounts or *balances* of the asset and liability accounts and the capital account as of the conclusion of the accounting procedures on a certain date such as December 31 of a particular year. The income statement is a record of the *balances* of the various income and expense accounts after the com-

* This subject is contained in another book by the present author, Accounting for Non-accountants. New York: New York University Press, 1957.

pletion of the accounting for the period ended at the date
of its related balance sheet.

TERMINOLOGY

In recent years accountants have been improving the
terminology of accounting in order to make it more understandable. As a result, there is both a newer and an older
name for each of the financial statements, as has been mentioned. Also, as has been indicated, the terms *income* and
revenue are used as synonyms. Because the traditional word
income has been employed with so many different meanings
in economics, finance, accounting, business, and law, it is
the opinion of some that the word *revenue* should be used
in its place. Various writers, particularly in the academic
field, are now doing this and it may become the generally
accepted term in the future. But the word *income* is still
the one in common use in business. It has, therefore, been
retained in this book and used interchangeably with *revenue*.
Since both an older and a newer term are in use for other
concepts, as will be seen later, the reader will have to become familiar with the alternatives that are encountered in
business.

3. The Accrual Basis of Accounting

THE ULTIMATE objective of accounting is to aid in the management of a business by supplying vital information. This information is used by executives in judging not only the overall success of the enterprise but also the effectiveness of managerial policies and the efficiency of the various phases of operations. It is also used as the basis for operations planning and other managerial decisions. Most of the information supplied by the accountant is in the form of statements, the most comprehensive of which are those mentioned in Chapter 2: the balance sheet which reviews the assets, the liabilities, and the capital as of a certain date, thus showing financial position, and the income statement which reviews the income and expenses of the period ended at the date of the related balance sheet, thus measuring the results of the operations in the form of net income or net loss.

Business is organized for the purpose of earning income. Its measurement is, therefore, the central feature of accounting. Income for a certain period of time may be measured on either the cash basis or the accrual basis. The cash basis is so simple as hardly to require any knowledge of accounting. It consists of keeping a record of cash receipts from sales and disbursements for expenses. Under this method an excess of such receipts over disbursements during a certain period results in net income for that period, while an excess of such disbursements over receipts results in a net loss. As will be shown, this method of measuring income does not produce a useful estimate of performance and, therefore, its use is more or less limited to small retail businesses where the owner is in such close contact with all phases of operations that he does not require a better measure of performance. Therefore, unless otherwise stated, all further discussion of net income in this book will be on the accrual basis.

In computing the net income under the accrual method, the receipt and disbursement of cash is disregarded. When the business has sold goods or performed services for which it is entitled to receive payment, income is considered to have been earned to the extent of the sum involved. In like manner, expenses are recognized when they have been incurred, although they may not have been paid for. Thus the determination of the net income on the accrual basis requires the inclusion of all income earned, whether collected or not, and all expenses of the period incurred in order to earn that income, whether paid for or not. On the other hand, costs incurred in order to earn income in the future are excluded.

The accountant deducts from the income of each period the expenses considered applicable to that period. Most of these will have been incurred during the period but others, such as fixed asset costs, may have been incurred in prior periods. Also, he deducts expenses that will be incurred and losses that will be sustained in the future in connection with sales made during the period under review. The amounts of future expenses and losses are determined on the basis of estimates. These matters will be discussed in detail in the following chapters.

The objective of the accrual basis is thus to obtain a measure of the results of operations by allocating to each period the income, or revenue, logically attributable to the operations of that period and the amount of all costs and losses in connection with the earning of the income. This process is called in accounting *matching costs with revenue.*

Since this measurement of net income is the central feature of accounting, this process of matching costs with revenue is the central problem of accounting. How the accountant solves this problem will be demonstrated in Chapters 4–7.

4. Financial Statements of a Service Individual Proprietorship

THERE ARE THREE important types of business ownership organization: (1) the individual proprietorship, (2) the partnership, and (3) the corporation. Also, there are three important kinds of business: (1) a service business, (2) a merchandising business, and (3) a manufacturing business. The financial statements of a service business organized as an individual proprietorship will be discussed in this chapter, the financial statements of a merchandising business organized as a partnership will be discussed in Chapter 5, and the financial statements of a manufacturing business organized as a corporation will be discussed in Chapter 6. There will thus be illustrated statements as they would appear for each of the three types of ownership organization and three kinds of business.

THE INCOME STATEMENT

The income statement of Robert Stowell, who is in the trucking business, for year ended December 31, 1963, is shown on page 23. It is seen that he had two sources of income: delivery charges and rental charges. The deductions from the income are such expenses as are to be expected in a trucking business. In preparing financial statements, it is becoming customary to round off the amounts to the nearest dollar, thus omitting cents, as in this statement.

Mr. Stowell's statement is on the accrual basis. Therefore, the income is for services performed during 1963 but the

ROBERT STOWELL
INCOME STATEMENT
FOR YEAR ENDED DECEMBER 31, 1963

INCOME:

Delivery charges	$152,367	
Rental charges	6,208	
Total income		$158,575

EXPENSES:

Gasoline and oil	$ 8,245
Wages	67,508
Payroll taxes	3,350
Truck maintenance and repairs	6,162
Rent	7,200
Heat and light	912
Insurance	3,200
Interest	130
Telephone	875
Supplies	6,221
Miscellaneous expense	3,690
Depreciation of trucks	10,345
Depreciation of furniture and equipment	862
Bad debts	153

Total expenses	118,853
Net income for the year	$ 39,722

sums indicated were not necessarily collected during that year. In fact, the collections made in 1963 included amounts for services rendered during 1962, some during 1963, and even some for services to be performed during 1964 paid for in advance. In similar manner, among the sums indicated as expenses, or deductions from income, there are included some that were paid for during 1963, some that were paid for in prior years, and some not yet paid for or even incurred. These matters will now be discussed.

DEPRECIATION

The fixed assets are acquired by a business to be used in carrying on its activities for the purpose of earning income. Their cost is, therefore, one of the regular expenses of the business and is deducted from income, as are the other expenses.

There, however, is a difference between this expense and others such as rent and electricity which belong to the period in which they are incurred. The fixed assets are usually employed over a considerable period of time. Trucks might last three years, furniture might be usable over a period of ten years, and a building might be used for thirty, forty, fifty years or more. Therefore, it would not provide management with a good measure of the results of operations if among the expenses of a certain year the total cost of the property and equipment purchased during the year were deducted from the income of that year. It produces a better measure of the results of operations if a part of the cost of such assets is apportioned to each of the years in which they are employed.

The allocation of a portion of the cost of the various kinds of property and equipment as an expense in the years in which they are used in the business, and thus producing income, presents a problem to which accountants have given considerable attention. Obviously, it is not possible to determine precisely, in terms of money, to what extent an asset has physically deteriorated during each year.

The way the matter is treated is to make the apportionment of the cost to successive years on some reasonable basis. The basis commonly used is that of the estimated useful life of the asset, that is, the number of years that it will be used by the business for the purpose of earning income, and to consider a portion of the cost of the asset an expense of each year. This expense is known as *depreciation*.

For example, if a machine should be purchased for $100 and it is estimated that it will be used for ten years, then one tenth of the cost, or $10, will be considered an expense of each of ten successive years. This is called the *straight-line method* of depreciation.

A second method is the *declining-balance method* whereby each year's depreciation is calculated on the cost of the asset minus the accumulated depreciation of the previous years. If this method were applied to the above illustration, the depreciation for the second year would be 10 per cent of $90, or $9; and so forth.

A third method, in use in connection with such assets as machinery, is that of computing depreciation in proportion to the number of hours the machines have been in operation during a year. This is called the *machine-hour method*. The rate is obtained by estimating a certain number of dollars of cost per hour.

Still another method is known as the *sum-of-the-years'-digits method*. It can best be explained by an illustration. If the asset to be depreciated has an estimated life of four years, the digits 1, 2, 3, and 4 are added. The total is 10. Starting with the last digit, the depreciation rate for the first year will be four tenths or 40 per cent, the second year, 30 per cent, the third year, 20 per cent, and the fourth, 10 per cent. This method gives the highest depreciation deduction for the first year with diminishing deductions for the following years.

Thus in the matter of the cost of fixed assets, an illustration is provided of an expense incurred and paid for in a period prior to its deduction from income.

In the case of Robert Stowell, the fixed assets had been purchased before 1963. His income statement shows that $10,345 of the cost of his trucks and $862 of the cost of the furniture and equipment were assigned as a deduction from the 1963 income.

ACCOUNTING DEPRECIATION AND PHYSICAL DEPRECIATION

There is not necessarily any close correspondence between the accounting depreciation and the physical depreciation or deterioration of the fixed assets. It is an ideal to have the accounting depreciation coincide with the physical depreciation and every effort is made toward this ideal. But as it is not humanly possible to foretell exactly the length of the useful life of an asset, all that is expected of accounting depreciation is that it will coincide reasonably with physical depreciation. Sometimes an asset may still render useful service after it has been fully depreciated in the accounting records. This fact does not disturb the accountant because he does not expect the accounting depreciation and physical depreciation to coincide precisely.

Since the government is interested in depreciation in connection with deductions made for income tax purposes, the rate to be used for each kind of asset is given in a pamphlet issued by the Bureau of Internal Revenue. These rates are intended as guides and may be modified to suit unusual situations.

ACCOUNTING DEPRECIATION A MISNOMER

As used in accounting the word *depreciation* is a misnomer. The word that would more correctly express what the accountant does is *amortization*: the extinguishment of the record of cost, as the asset is used up. Depreciation signifies decline in value. The accountant, however, when computing depreciation is not concerned with the present worth or market value of fixed assets but with the apportionment of their cost as a deduction from income. Since the word *depreciation* has been the accepted term used to describe this function for many years, it is difficult to make a change in terminology.

BAD DEBTS

Because it is desired on the accrual basis of accounting to place in the income and expense record of each period what logically belongs to the period, the loss on uncollectible receivables is placed in the period in which the sales from which such receivables resulted were made. Obviously, at the end of an accounting period it is not possible to state which of the unpaid accounts will not be collected. Therefore, a deduction from income for the loss on uncollectible accounts is estimated more or less on the basis of past experience, commonly as a certain percentage of the total of the receivables. In the case of Robert Stowell under consideration, it was estimated that 1 per cent, or $153, of his accounts receivable amounting to $15,278 would not be collected.

The bad debts estimate is an illustration of the deduction from income of an expense, or loss, that has not yet occurred but is considered as belonging to the period under review.

ACCRUED INCOME

As of the end of a period, certain income may have been earned but the conditions with respect to this income may be such that it has not been recorded. For example, in the case of Mr. Stowell a contract to transport certain goods was entered into but as of December 31, 1963, the job had not been completed. Upon completion, the sum due Mr. Stowell from this client would be added to the accounts receivable and a record made of the income earned on the job. It is, however, logical to include the amount earned on the completed portion of the job in the income of 1963. This amounted to $385, which sum was added to the income from delivery charges in compiling the income statement.

Accrued income thus provides an illustration of income included as belonging to the period under review although not only not collected but also not yet included in the accounts receivable.

DEFERRED INCOME

A business may during an accounting period have received payment for services to be performed in the next period. During 1963 Mr. Stowell was paid such income in advance amounting to $250. When this sum was received, it was added to the cash and also added to the record of income. But since this income was not earned during 1963 it was deferred by deducting it from the recorded income in compiling the income statement.

It is thus seen that if income is paid to a business during a certain period but not earned, it is not, on the accrual basis, included in the income for that period reported in the income statement but is *deferred* to the future.

ACCRUED EXPENSES

As of the end of a period, expenses may have been incurred but not recorded. For example, December 31, 1963 was a Tuesday. Since Mr. Stowell pays his employees on Saturdays, the wages for December 30 and 31 would not be recorded until January 4, 1964, the payday for the week. However, on the accrual basis, the wages accrued for the last two days of December, amounting to $575, have been included in the wages for 1963 amounting to $67,508 shown in the income statement. Another expense accrued was interest amounting to $20.

Accrued expenses thus provide an illustration of expenses included as belonging to the period under review although not only not paid for but also not included in the accounts payable.

PREPAID EXPENSES

During an accounting period a business may have paid in advance for expenses that belong to a future period or may have recorded a liability for them. For example, during 1963 Mr. Stowell paid an insurance premium covering insurance for three years. Therefore, only part of the recorded insurance expense belongs to 1963. Accordingly, that part belonging to the future amounting to $1,250 as of December 31, 1963 was a *prepaid expense* and was deferred by deducting it from the recorded insurance expense of the period. Similarly, discount, or interest paid in advance, on a promissory note given to a bank for a loan was deferred in the amount of $40, as also was the cost of supplies purchased and not used, amounting to $863.

Prepaid expenses thus provide an illustration of expenses either paid for or included in the accounts payable but not belonging to the period under review and, therefore, not included in the expenses reported in the income statement.

ADJUSTMENTS

In order to obtain the income and expense figures on the accrual basis it is necessary for the accountant to review the records at the end of each accounting period and to make adjustment of the recorded income and expenses to

(1) include depreciation expense;
(2) include the estimated loss on bad debts;
(3) increase the income for income accrued;
(4) decrease the income for income to be deferred;
(5) increase the expenses for expenses accrued; and
(6) decrease the expenses for expenses to be deferred, or, as commonly called, expenses prepaid.

This process is referred to as making the periodic adjustments.

THE BALANCE SHEET

The balance sheet of Robert Stowell as of December 31, 1963 is shown on pages 30–31. It will be observed that this statement consists of two sections: one for the assets and the other for the equities—the liabilities and the capital. It thus conforms to that axiomatic or fundamental equation of accounting mentioned in Chapter 1. The assets, $62,201, equal the liabilities, $10,592, plus the capital, $51,609.

The balance sheet shows the financial position of the business since it indicates the position or amount of each asset, each liability, and the capital.

CURRENT ASSETS

In the balance sheet the assets are divided into sections for current assets and fixed assets. The current assets are placed in the order of liquidity. The most liquid asset is cash

ROBERT STOWELL
BALANCE SHEET
DECEMBER 31, 1963

Assets

CURRENT ASSETS:

Cash			$ 6,872
Accounts receivable		$15,278	
Less Estimated bad debts		169	15,109
Accrued income:			
Delivery charges			385
Prepaid expenses:			
Insurance		$ 1,250	
Interest		40	
Supplies		863	2,153
Total current assets			$24,519

FIXED ASSETS:

Trucks	$50,700		
Less Accumulated depreciation	21,250	$29,450	
Furniture and equipment	$12,482		
Less Accumulated depreciation	4,250	8,232	
Total fixed assets			37,682
			$62,201

Liabilities and Capital

CURRENT LIABILITIES:

Notes payable			$ 3,500
Accounts payable			6,247
Accrued expenses:			
Wages		$575	
Interest		20	595
Total current liabilities			$10,342

DEFERRED INCOME:

Delivery charges		250
Total liabilities		$10,592

ROBERT STOWELL, CAPITAL		51,609
		$62,201

because it is most readily converted into other kinds of assets. In the case of Robert Stowell, the next in order of liquidity is the accounts receivable which in the course of time will be collected and thus converted into cash. Note that the bad debts estimate is deducted from the accounts receivable, the difference being the estimated cash realizable amount of the receivables. Next comes the accrued income, explained above, representing earnings on a contract for delivery services not yet completed. This will become an account receivable upon completion of the work. The prepaid expenses, which have been discussed above, are placed at the end of the current asset section by some accountants, as here shown, but other accountants place them in a separate section after the fixed assets.

FIXED ASSETS

There are no prescribed rules for the order in which the fixed assets are to be placed. Because they vary from one kind of business to another, the accountant uses his discretion with respect to the order in which they are listed. The tendency, however, is to place them in the order of importance.

Note that the accumulated depreciation to date is deducted from each fixed asset. The balance sheet thus shows, for example, that the trucks cost $50,700, that of this amount $21,250 has been deducted from income earned up to December 31, 1963, and that $29,450 of the cost of the trucks will be deducted from future income. This difference of $29,450 is the unamortized portion of the cost and is commonly called the book value of the asset. It, of course, has no relation to the market value of the trucks.

CURRENT LIABILITIES

Among the liabilities, the current liabilities are placed first, followed by the long-term liabilities, if any. There are no long-term liabilities in the case of Robert Stowell.

The current liabilities are placed in the order of urgency. Notes payable are a more urgent debt than accounts payable since they must be paid precisely on the day they mature, otherwise the credit standing of the business would become impaired. Next in order come the accrued expenses, already explained, which in due time will become accounts payable.

The deferred income, according to the facts in the case mentioned above, will no doubt be collected during the coming year. Although it represents an obligation to a client, it does not require a payment. For this reason it is not included in the current liabilities.

CAPITAL

The capital or equity of the owner is, as has already been explained, the excess of assets over liabilities, or what would be the total of the assets if all liabilities were liquidated. In the case of Robert Stowell the assets are stated at $62,201, in which the creditors have an equity of $10,592 and the owner an equity of $51,609.

EFFECT OF THE PERIODIC ADJUSTMENTS

Let us now review the effect of the periodic adjustments on the financial statements.

Depreciation. The depreciation expense for the year for each fixed asset is shown in the income statement and is included in the accumulated depreciation deducted from the cost of the asset in the balance sheet.

Estimated bad debts. The estimated loss on bad debts is shown in the income statement. This amount is deducted from the accounts receivable in the balance sheet. In the balance sheet before us, although the anticipated loss as of December 31, 1963 is $153, the amount deducted is $169. The difference indicates that the estimate at December 31, 1962 exceeded the actual loss by $16, which amount is carried forward. Such a difference often occurs for it cannot be expected that the estimate will be precise.

Accrued income. This represents income earned but as of the close of business at the balance sheet date had not been recorded. Since it is in the nature of an amount to be received at some time in the future it was added to the assets in the balance sheet; and because this asset was acquired through earnings, its amount was added to the income reported in the income statement.

Prepaid expenses. These expenses were paid for during

1963 but as of December 31, 1963 the business had not received the benefit from the payments. They thus represent good and valuable assets from which the business will receive benefit in the future. Their amounts were, therefore, not included in the expenses reported in the income statement. They will be converted from assets into expenses in the future when the insurance expires, the note on which the interest applies matures, and the supplies are used up.

Accrued expenses. These expenses, because they were found to belong to 1963, were included in those reported in the income statement. The liability for them is shown in the balance sheet.

Deferred income. This income, which was received for services not yet performed, was not included in the income reported in the income statement. The obligation to the client for the sum paid in advance is reported in the balance sheet.

It is accordingly seen that all periodic adjustments affect both the income statement and the balance sheet.

5. Financial Statements of a Merchandising Partnership

THE INCOME STATEMENT

THE IMPORTANT difference between the income statement of a merchandising business and that of a service business lies in the area of the revenue, or gross income, that is, the income before the deduction of the expenses of operating the business to obtain the net income.

It has been shown that in a service business there is one or more sources of revenue. The total of each of these is readily available in the accounting records. In a merchandising business the gross income, or gross profit, or gross margin, as it is variously called, is obtained by deducting the *cost of the goods sold* from what was realized from the sale of merchandise, after deducting the returns, allowances, and cash discounts allowed, that is, the *net sales*. This is demonstrated in the income statement of the partnership of Turner and Williams on pages 36–37. The statement shows that the net sales for 1963 amounted to $183,236. After deducting from this the cost of the goods sold, amounting to $74,911, there remained a gross profit of $108,325.

COST OF GOODS SOLD

The cost of goods sold is obtained by taking into consideration a number of factors. When to the inventory of merchandise at the beginning of the period there is added

35

TURNER AND WILLIAMS
INCOME STATEMENT
FOR YEAR ENDED DECEMBER 31, 1963

Sales			$185,726
Less Returns and allowances		$ 962	
Cash discounts		1,528	2,490
Sales, net of returns, allowances, and discounts			$183,236
COST OF GOODS SOLD			
Inventory, January 1		$ 38,254	
Purchases	$86,327		
Freight and cartage inward	286		
	$86,613		
Less Returns and allowances	$ 473		
Cash discounts	1,798	2,271	84,342
Total goods to be accounted for			$122,596
Less Inventory, December 31			47,685
Cost of goods sold			74,911
Gross profit on sales			$108,325

SELLING, GENERAL, AND ADMINISTRATIVE EXPENSES:

Salaries	$ 35,285	
Payroll taxes	1,624	
Rent	10,800	
Insurance	507	
Delivery expense	5,386	
Supplies	3,654	
Telephone and telegraph	620	
Miscellaneous expense	4,256	
Depreciation of furniture and fixtures	925	
Bad debts	354	
		63,411
		$ 44,914

OTHER EXPENSES:

Interest		385
		$ 44,529

OTHER INCOME:

Rent	$ 360	
Interest	15	375
Net income for the year		$ 44,904

the cost of the goods purchased during the period plus the cost of freight and cartage on these goods, and there is then deducted the price of the goods returned to the vendor and the cash discounts taken on the goods purchased, the result is the cost of the goods to be accounted for. Of these, some were sold and some remain in stock. Now, if from the cost of goods to be accounted for the cost of those in stock is deducted, the difference will be the cost of those that were sold.

NET INCOME FOR THE YEAR

After deducting the expenses from and adding any other income to the gross profit, the net income for the year is obtained.

Note in the case of Turner and Williams the classification of the expenses into *selling, general, and administrative expenses* and *other expenses*. Interest expense (the cost of obtaining money) and special kinds of expenses and losses are classified as *other expenses* because they are matters not connected with operating the business. The *other income*, not being part of the income from regular operations, is placed in a separate section at the end of the statement.

THE INVENTORY: PERIODIC METHOD

The dollar amount of the merchandise inventory is an important factor in calculating the gross profit. There are two types of inventory procedure in use: (1) the *periodic inventory* and (2) the *perpetual inventory*.

The periodic inventory procedure consists of making a physical count of all articles in stock at least once a year at the end of the accounting period. At all other times during the year there is no complete information available on the amount of the stock of goods. The periodic inventory procedure is simple and relatively inexpensive. It is, therefore, the type most commonly used, particularly in small businesses. The inventory is recorded on inventory sheets which show the various items in stock and the number of units of each. The units are multiplied by prices to obtain the dollar amounts.

A problem arises when a change in the replacement price has taken place since certain of the items in the inventory were acquired. Accordingly, the question arises whether the units shall be priced at the cost price or at the current market price. The answer to this question is found in the generally accepted rule that the items in the inventory shall be priced at *cost or market, whichever is lower*. Therefore, if the market price at the date of the inventory has declined, the market price is used. But if the market price has risen, the cost price is used.

The effect of the lower of cost or market rule is to take a loss when the market price has declined but not to take a gain when it has risen. Such losses and gains are unrealized or "paper" losses and gains since a gain or loss is not realized until an article is sold. The fact that an unrealized loss is recognized while an unrealized gain is not does not conform entirely with logical reasoning; but the accounting profession defends its position by explaining that it is prompted by *conservatism*, an attitude which fears to overstate profits but is not so fearful of understating them. It is in line with the principle of the accrual basis that all foreseeable losses should be provided for, as, for instance, the foreseeable loss on bad debts, although in the case of the merchandise inventory the principle is stretched somewhat to include losses that may or may not occur.

The application of the cost or market, whichever is lower rule is not always feasible in practice, particularly in a manufacturing business. However, it is the generally accepted rule where no other procedures have been adopted.

PERPETUAL INVENTORY

Under the periodic inventory procedure it is necessary to make a physical count of the stock in order to determine the net income. Since the making of a physical count of all the stock is in most cases a time-consuming and laborious task, it is not feasible to do this more frequently than once a year. Consequently, the net income can be determined only once a year.

However, in some lines of business it is essential to have more frequent information on how matters are going. This is especially true in a manufacturing enterprise, for in this type of business the management must constantly be supplied with current data in order to exercise proper control. In such cases a system is used whereby a record is kept of all goods coming into and going out of the stockroom. There is thus a constant or perpetual record of the merchandise in stock. Where such a perpetual inventory is available, it is possible to prepare an income statement frequently, such as at the end of each month.

In spite of the fact that when a perpetual inventory system is used there is a constant record of goods in stock, the book inventory must periodically be verified by a physical count because goods become lost, are stolen, or they deteriorate. The dollar amount of any missing goods will be treated as a loss.

DETERMINATION OF COST

In applying the cost or market, whichever is lower rule in a period of changing prices, the cost of a particular commodity in an inventory may depend on the method used with respect to assigning the cost prices to the goods taken out of stock. As goods are issued the cost prices may be assigned beginning with the first price at which the goods were purchased. When the quantity issued equals the quantity purchased at this price, the next price is assigned, and so forth. This is called the first-in, first-out method, commonly referred to as FIFO. However, the cost may be assigned beginning with the price of the last units that went into stock. This is known as the last-in, first-out method, referred to as LIFO. Either method is acceptable for income tax purposes.

It should be noted that "first out" and "last out" refer to the order in which costs are assigned to goods and not to the goods themselves. To avoid deterioration, the items placed in stock first will usually be taken out first although the last price may be assigned to them.

Another method is the average cost method whereby the costs are assigned at the average cost of those in stock. Still other methods are in use but they are not commonly encountered.

In order to illustrate and compare the operation of the FIFO, LIFO, and average cost methods, let us use the following data with respect to the receipt and issue of a certain commodity.

1964
June   5 Received 200 units @ $.20
      11 Issued 50 units
      17 Received 100 units @ $.21
      25 Issued 200 units
      30 Issued 30 units

These data are shown on page 42 as they would be recorded under each of the three methods in a perpetual inventory record. Note that each method produces a different figure for the 20 units on hand on June 30, 1964. From this it is seen that different accounting procedures produce different results. Why this fact should not cause concern will be discussed in Chapter 7.

The LIFO method has become the preferred method because by assigning prices which are as nearly as possible the current ones it places the cost of goods sold in the income statement on approximately the same price level as the sales figure which is more or less on the current price level. The average price method is not popular because it involves the burden of a mathematical calculation every time a new price is introduced.

THE BALANCE SHEET

The balance sheet of the firm of Turner and Williams is found on page 43. This statement is arranged horizontally with the assets to the left and the liabilities and capital to the right. Some accountants prefer this arrangement to the vertical arrangement shown in Chapter 4.

The difference between the balance sheet of an individual proprietorship and a partnership is that the balance sheet of an individual proprietorship contains a single capital item while the balance sheet of a partnership indicates the capital or equity of each partner. In the case of Turner and Williams the capitals are equal.

The merchandise inventory is, as stated in Chapter 1, a current asset. Note that in the case of Turner and Williams the inventory is stated on the basis of the lower of cost or market according to the LIFO method. The arrangement from cash to merchandise, the order of liquidity, is sometimes referred to as the "trading cycle" for the movement of assets is from merchandise, when sold, to receivables,

FIFO METHOD

Date		RECEIVED			ISSUED			BALANCE		
		Units	Price	Amount	Units	Price	Amount	Units	Price	Amount
1964 June	5	200	.20	40.00				200	.20	40.00
	11				50	.20	10.00	150	.20	30.00
	17	100	.21	21.00				150	.20	30.00
								100	.21	21.00
	25				150	.20	30.00			
					50	.21	10.50	50	.21	10.50
	30				30	.21	6.30	20	.21	4.20

LIFO METHOD

Date		RECEIVED			ISSUED			BALANCE		
		Units	Price	Amount	Units	Price	Amount	Units	Price	Amount
1964 June	5	200	.20	40.00				200	.20	40.00
	11				50	.20	10.00	150	.20	30.00
	17	100	.21	21.00				150	.20	30.00
								100	.21	21.00
	25				100	.21	21.00			
					100	.20	20.00	50	.20	10.00
	30				30	.20	6.00	20	.20	4.00

AVERAGE METHOD

Date		RECEIVED			ISSUED			BALANCE		
		Units	Price	Amount	Units	Price	Amount	Units	Price	Amount
1964 June	5	200	.20	40.00				200	.20	40.00
	11				50	.20	10.00	150	.20	30.00
	17	100	.21	21.00				250	.204	51.00
	25				200	.204	40.80	150	.204	10.20
	30				30	.204	6.12	20	.204	4.08

42

TURNER AND WILLIAMS
BALANCE SHEET
DECEMBER 31, 1963

Assets

CURRENT ASSETS:

Cash		$ 5,162	
Notes receivable		500	
Accounts receivable	$20,862		
Less Allowance for bad debts	389	20,473	
Merchandise inventory (at the lower of cost or market according to the LIFO method)		47,685	
Prepaid expenses		938	
Total current assets			$74,758

FIXED ASSETS:

Furniture and fixtures	$ 9,470		
Less Allowance for depreciation	3,654		
Total fixed assets		5,816	
			$80,574

Liabilities and Capital

CURRENT LIABILITIES:

Notes payable (bank)	$ 2,500
Accounts payable	6,325
Accrued expenses	1,297
Total current liabilities	$10,122
R. J. TURNER, CAPITAL	35,226
A. L. WILLIAMS, CAPITAL	35,226
	$80,574

which when collected are converted into cash; and then cash is converted into new merchandise as it is purchased.

The expression *allowance for bad debts* used in the balance sheet is preferred by some accountants instead of *estimated bad debts*, as is also *allowance for depreciation* instead of *accumulated depreciation*.

It is apparent that no loss on uncollectible notes receivable is anticipated by Turner and Williams since the estimated loss is deducted from the accounts receivable alone.

A business does not necessarily have all of the four types of accruals and deferrals that have been discussed. Turner and Williams have prepaid expenses and accrued expenses but no accrued income or deferred income. In fact, almost every business has some prepaid and accrued expenses at the balance sheet date but, except in certain lines of business, accrued and deferred income are relatively uncommon.

Note that the prepaid and accrued expenses are stated in the balance sheet of Turner and Williams in total. They are often so stated because their sums are relatively not material.

6. Financial Statements of a Manufacturing Corporation

THE INCOME STATEMENT

THE INCOME STATEMENT of a manufacturing business differs primarily from that of a merchandising business in that it requires a more elaborate computation to obtain the cost of goods sold. A merchandising business purchases the goods to be sold in finished condition, ready for sale. The cost of the goods purchased for resale during a certain period is indicated in the cost of goods sold section of its income statement by the item *purchases* as shown on page 36.

A manufacturing business purchases materials and manufactures them into finished products to be sold. Therefore, in place of the item *purchases* of the income statement of a merchandising business the income statement of a manufacturing business shows the *cost of goods manufactured*, thus indicating the cost of acquisition of goods in that type of business.

Because of the conversion of materials into finished products, a manufacturing business usually has, as of the close of business on the last day of an accounting period, three distinct inventories. It has (1) an inventory of *materials*, sometimes referred to as raw materials, (2) an inventory of *finished goods*, and (3) an inventory of *work in process*, that is, partly finished goods.

Since the cost of goods sold section of the income statement of a manufacturing business tends to become large, it is commonly prepared in the form of a schedule appended

LEMINTO CORPORATION
SCHEDULE OF COST OF GOODS SOLD
FOR YEAR ENDED JUNE 30, 1964

Inventory of finished goods, July 1, 1963			$ 225,372
Inventory of work in process, July 1, 1963		$	10,762
MATERIALS:			
Inventory, July 1, 1963		$109,798	
Purchases		828,659	
Freight and cartage inward		1,250	
		$939,707	
Less Returns and allowances	$3,863		
Cash discounts	7,649	11,512	
		$928,195	
Less Inventory, June 30, 1964		102,793	
Materials used			825,402
DIRECT LABOR			385,437

46

MANUFACTURING OVERHEAD:

Supplies	$ 18,782	
Insurance—Factory	2,549	
Taxes—Factory	8,615	
Gas and electricity—Factory	9,241	
Depreciation of factory building	48,942	
Repairs to factory building	10,629	
Depreciation of machinery and equipment	11,905	
Repairs to machinery	3,640	
Indirect labor	42,485	
Payroll taxes—Factory	17,691	
Miscellaneous factory expense	8,485	
Total manufacturing overhead		182,964
Total manufacturing costs		$1,404,565
Less Inventory of work in process, June 30, 1964		30,540
Cost of goods manufactured		1,374,025
		$1,599,397
Less Inventory of finished goods, June 30, 1964		362,795
Cost of goods sold		$1,236,602

to the income statement and the cost of goods sold is stated in the income statement in total.

The schedule of cost of goods sold of the Leminto Corporation for year ended June 30, 1964 is shown on pages 46–47. It is seen that the cost of goods manufactured consists of three elements: (1) *direct materials*, (2) *direct labor*, and (3) *manufacturing overhead*.

Direct materials are those that constitute an appreciable part of the finished product; for example, the cloth in making clothing.

Direct labor is the name given to the labor applied to the materials placed into the production process such as, in the case of the manufacturer of clothing, the labor of the cutters and sewers.

Manufacturing overhead comprises the countless expenses in connection with the manufacturing processes that cannot be identified with the products. They include such items as the depreciation and maintenance of the building and machinery, the taxes on the property, and the electricity, water, and gas consumed in operations.

The manufacturing overhead includes the labor of such workers as foremen, repairmen, cleaners, and engineers. Their labor, known as *indirect labor*, although not applied directly to the products, nevertheless aids in production.

Also included in the manufacturing overhead are materials not identified with the products, such as the oil used to lubricate the machinery and the rags used for wiping. These are known as *indirect materials* or *supplies*.

The direct materials and direct labor are classified as *direct costs* and the manufacturing overhead as *indirect costs*. The total of the direct materials and direct labor is often referred to as the *prime cost*.

The cost of goods sold thus consists of:

> Initial inventory of finished goods
> Plus Cost of goods manufactured
> Less Final inventory of finished goods

The cost of goods manufactured consists of:

> Initial inventory of work in process
> Plus Cost of direct material used
>   Cost of direct labor
>   Manufacturing overhead
> Less Final inventory of work in process

The cost of the direct materials used consists of:

> Initial inventory of materials
> Plus Purchases of materials
>   Freight and cartage on materials
> Less Returns and allowances
>   Cash discounts
>   Materials used indirectly
>   Final inventory of materials

The income statement of the Leminto Corporation is illustrated on pages 50–51. Note the showing of the cost of goods sold in total; also that the selling expenses have been classified separately from the general and administrative expenses. Since this is obviously a larger business than those whose statements have been previously reviewed, the sales function is clearly separated from the administrative function and thus more susceptible of observation and control by the management.

Among the *other expenses* are the following three items which further illustrate the application of the accrual basis:

Amortization of bond discount. On July 1, 1962, the corporation issued $100,000 first-mortgage, 5-year, 6 per cent, sinking-fund bonds at 92. The discount of $8,000 is an expense of the business which on the accrual basis is amortized over the life of the bond issue, that is, over 5 years, at the rate of 20 per cent per annum. The expense is thus apportioned $1,600 to each of the five years.

Provision for warranty. The corporation gives a 5-year warranty on its products. If in that time any defects occur, barring abuse, it makes the necessary repairs. The cost of maintaining this warranty is an expense of the business. In accordance with the accrual basis, each year there is made a deduction from income for the cost of maintaining the warranty on the products sold during the year. It is, of course, made on the basis of an estimate, similar to the deduction from income of the estimated loss on bad debts.

Provision for fire loss. The corporation insures its property against fire but not for 100 per cent of its replacement cost. Each year it has to bear some loss not covered by insurance. Therefore, provision is made for this loss, in anticipation, by a deduction from income on the basis of an estimate.

LEMINTO CORPORATION
INCOME STATEMENT
FOR YEAR ENDED JUNE 30, 1964

Sales			$2,297,462
Less Returns and allowances		$ 12,640	
Cash discounts		22,756	35,396
Sales, net of returns, allowances, and discounts			$2,262,066
COST OF GOODS SOLD (*See Schedule*)			1,236,602
Gross profit on sales			$1,025,464
SELLING EXPENSES:			
Sales office rent		$ 24,000	
Salesmen's salaries		228,259	
Payroll taxes—Selling		9,618	
Depreciation of salesroom furniture		1,792	
Delivery expense		32,490	
Freight and cartage outward		2,592	
Advertising		85,283	
Miscellaneous selling expense		12,995	
Total selling expenses			397,029
			$ 628,435
GENERAL AND ADMINISTRATIVE EXPENSES:			
General office rent		$ 26,400	
General office salaries		104,182	
Payroll taxes—General		4,275	
Depreciation of general office furniture		1,526	

50

Office supplies	10,340	
Insurance—General	1,182	
Bad debts	3,500	
Postage	1,526	
Miscellaneous general expense	5,245	
Total general and administrative expenses		158,176
		$ 470,259

OTHER EXPENSES:

Interest	$ 5,650	
Amortization of bond discount	1,600	
Provision for warranty	30,000	
Provision for fire loss	10,250	
Loss on sale of equipment	1,375	
Total other expenses		48,875
		$ 421,384

OTHER INCOME:

Profit on sale of securities	$ 1,280	
Interest on investments	1,842	
Income from sale of waste	2,517	
Total other income		5,639
Net income before federal income taxes		$ 427,023
Federal income taxes		216,552
Net income for the year		$ 210,471

FEDERAL INCOME TAXES

Federal income taxes is the last deduction from income in the corporate income statement. This is so because it is necessary to compute the net income before federal income taxes for the taxes are based on this figure. The plural *taxes* is used because there are two: the normal tax and the surtax.

THE BALANCE SHEET

The balance sheet of the Leminto Corporation as of June 30, 1964 is found on pages 54–57. The corporation uses a fiscal year ending June 30. There is a growing use of an accounting or fiscal year other than the calendar year. In some lines of business there has been established a uniform fiscal year in accordance with a principle known as the "natural business year." The fiscal year selected is the most logical one for the business: when the inventory reaches its lowest point and a new cycle begins. For example, department stores have selected January 31.

CLASSIFICATION OF ASSETS

In a business that has a diversity of assets the two classifications of current and fixed are not adequate. Therefore, the classification *fixed assets* is not used and the noncurrent assets are subdivided into various groups, as seen in the balance sheet of the Leminto Corporation herewith.

MARKETABLE SECURITIES

Many corporations that have funds available not needed for current operations but which may be needed in the not too distant future invest them temporarily in readily marketable securities, most commonly United States Government bonds. This enables the business to obtain income from these funds while at the same time being able to reconvert the securities into cash whenever necessary. Such temporary investments in marketable securities are listed in the balance sheet immediately after the cash; they are in the nature of "near-cash." Marketable securities are usually stated at cost. If there is any appreciable difference between cost and market quotations, market is stated parenthetically.

INVENTORIES

A distinctive feature of the balance sheet of a manufacturing business is that there are three inventories: materials, work in process, and finished goods. Although the traditional principle of the lower of cost or market may readily be applied to the materials inventory, it is often not feasible to apply it to the finished goods and work in process inventories which are then stated at cost.

PROPERTY, PLANT, AND EQUIPMENT

The investment in property, plant, and equipment of a manufacturing business is usually relatively large. Under this head the various types of assets are listed at cost less accumulated depreciation. Cost includes all costs in connection with acquisition of the asset; also any improvements and betterments which have been made since its acquisition. This applies particularly to such assets as buildings.

Note that in the case of the Leminto Corporation the depreciation accumulated to date is stated simply as depreciation—another variation in usage.

GOODWILL

Goodwill arises upon the acquisition of a business for which a greater sum is paid than the stated amount of its tangible property, usually because the business has unusual earning power. Goodwill is classified as an *intangible asset*. It is often listed as an independent item, as in the balance sheet of the Leminto Corporation.

LEMINTO CORPORATION
BALANCE SHEET
JUNE 30, 1964

Assets

CURRENT ASSETS:

Cash		$ 242,163
Marketable securities, at cost (market $120,075)		122,650
Accounts receivable	$180,794	
Less Estimated bad debts	3,616	177,178
Inventories		
Materials (at the lower of LIFO cost or market)		102,793
Work in process (at cost)		30,540
Finished goods (at LIFO cost)		362,795
Prepaid expenses		9,716
Total current assets		$1,047,835

PROPERTY, PLANT, AND EQUIPMENT:

Land			$562,000
Factory building	$1,327,546		
Less Depreciation	362,850		964,696
Machinery and equipment	$ 104,682		
Less Depreciation	17,385		87,297
Trucks	$ 12,460		
Less Depreciation	3,487		8,973
Salesroom furniture	$ 13,370		
Less Depreciation	1,425		11,945
General office furniture	$ 14,297		
Less Depreciation	845		13,452
Total property, plant, and equipment			1,648,363

GOODWILL

			1

DEFERRED CHARGES:

Bond discount	$ 4,800		
Organization expense	3,250		
Total deferred charges			8,050

OTHER ASSETS:

Accounts receivable (not current)	$ 6,000		
Miscellaneous advances and deposits	8,500		
Total other assets			14,500
			$2,818,749

Liabilities and Capital

CURRENT LIABILITIES:

Accounts payable		$ 97,365
Accrued expenses		15,271
Dividends payable		102,500
Federal income taxes payable		216,552
Sinking fund payment due July 1, 1964		20,000
Total current liabilities		$ 451,688

FUNDED DEBT:

First mortgage, 5-year, 6% sinking-fund bonds, due July 1, 1967	$ 80,000	
Less Sinking fund payment due July 1, 1964 (above)	20,000	
Total funded debt		60,000

RESERVES:

Reserve for warranty	$ 52,780	
Reserve for fire loss	18,640	
Total reserves		71,420

CAPITAL STOCK:

7% cumulative preferred stock, par $100

Authorized and issued, 2,000 shares .... $ 200,000

Common stock, no par, stated value $5

Authorized, 500,000 shares

Issued, 300,000 shares 1,500,000

Total capital stock $1,700,000

RETAINED EARNINGS (restricted $30,000 because of

purchase of stock for the treasury) 165,641

CAPITAL IN EXCESS OF STATED VALUE OF

COMMON STOCK 300,000

$2,165,641

Less Treasury stock—Common

5,000 shares, at cost 30,000

Total capital 2,135,641

$2,818,749

At the time a business is acquired, the measurement of its goodwill in dollars may be a reasonable one. However, since earning power fluctuates, it is not to be expected that the stated amount will continue to be a satisfactory measure. Hence, it is quite common to remove or "write off" the goodwill with a corresponding deduction from the capital. Sometimes when this is done $1 is left to indicate that the business possesses goodwill but takes a conservative attitude by not listing it at an appreciable figure, as in the case of the Leminto Corporation.

The rules of accounting prescribe that goodwill may be recorded only when a payment has been made in recognition of its existence. It might be mentioned here that goodwill is recorded in a partnership when a new partner, upon being admitted to the partnership, recognizes its existence and so is required to make a greater investment for an interest than he would if the goodwill were not recognized.

Other examples of intangible assets are: trademarks, copyrights, franchises, and patents. These are stated at cost of acquisition. In the case of patent rights, acquisition may be by purchase or by development by the business itself. The cost of these assets is amortized over their legal life.

DEFERRED CHARGES

Deferred charges are similar to prepaid expenses in that they are costs that have been incurred but are deferred to the future, that is, they will be deducted from future income. Some accountants make no distinction between deferred charges and prepaid expenses, listing both in the section for deferred charges. When a distinction is made the items classified as deferred charges are such as result from infrequent transactions: the discount on bonds issued and the cost involved in the organization of the corporation, commonly known as organization expense. Bond discount, as was stated above, is amortized over the life of the bond issue. Organization expense is usually amortized over an arbitrary period of time such as five years. In contrast to the deferred charges, the items classified as prepaid expenses are the more routine costs to be deferred, such as insurance and office supplies.

OTHER ASSETS

The classification *other assets* is used for all assets not classified elsewhere. It may include noncurrent receivables, deposits made with public utility companies, various sums set aside for special purposes, and so forth.

LONG-TERM LOANS

Long-term loans are listed in the balance sheet in a section following the current liabilities. They may be in the form of mortgage or debenture bonds, long-term notes, or mortgages on real estate. Mortgage bonds are secured by a lien on the corporation's property while debenture bonds are unsecured. Information regarding the maturity date and rate of interest should be given.

The process of combining various debts into one large debt or fund is known as *funding* the debts. And because the corporation frequently uses the money obtained through an issue of bonds to pay off various debts, the bonds of a corporation are commonly referred to as its *funded debt*.

DISCOUNT OR PREMIUM ON BONDS

Corporate bonds are most commonly disposed of through an investment banking house, or group of such houses known as a syndicate, who "underwrite" the issue, that is, they agree to buy it from the corporation at a certain price. The underwriters then sell the bonds to their clients at a higher price. But sometimes a bond issue is disposed of by direct sale to one investor such as an insurance company, thus eliminating the underwriters.

Bonds are sold by the corporation at par or at a discount or premium. They are usually disposed of to underwriters at a discount or premium. The discount or premium is arrived at by the underwriters through a variety of considerations such as the interest of the public in the issue, the expenses of marketing it, and their profit on the transaction.

It sometimes includes a precise adjustment of the stated interest rate. Because of differences in market conditions and marketing methods, industrial bonds are commonly disposed of at a discount and public utility bonds at a premium.

Discount on bonds is an expense of the corporation and, as has been shown, is amortized as a deduction from income over the life of the bond issue, the unamortized portion being treated as a deferred charge. Similarly, premium on bonds is a form of gain to the corporation and is amortized as an addition to income over the life of the bond issue. The unamortized portion is treated as deferred income.

SINKING FUND PAYMENTS

When *sinking fund bonds* are issued, periodic payments of an agreed sum are made by the corporation to the trustee who represents the bondholders. The trustee may either accumulate the sums paid in a *sinking fund* until the date of maturity of the bond issue, investing the money to earn interest which is added to the fund, or he may call bonds for redemption periodically, thus gradually reducing the corporation's funded debt. The latter plan is at present usually used.

From the statements of the Leminto Corporation it is seen that bonds were issued on July 1, 1962 in the amount of $100,000 and that they were issued at 92, meaning that for each $1,000 bond the corporation received $920. Thus the discount amounted to $4,800. As of June 30, 1964, two years had elapsed; therefore, through the operation of the sinking fund the first payment of $20,000 was made on July 1, 1963 and the second payment of $20,000, shown as a current liability in the balance sheet, would be made on July 1, 1964. The amortization of the discount for year ended June 30, 1964, $1,600, is shown as an expense in the income statement and, as already observed, the unamortized discount, $4,800, is shown as a deferred charge in the balance sheet.

Other types of bonds are issued with provision for gradual redemption. There are the *serial bonds* which are issued in series, each series of an issue being redeemable at a different date. Then there are *callable bonds* which may be called for redemption at the option of the corporation at any interest date, usually with the proviso that a premium will be paid to the bondholder when the bonds are called.

RESERVES FOR ANTICIPATED COSTS AND LOSSES

It is a principle of accounting that the accountant should provide by a deduction from income for all foreseeable costs and losses that can reasonably be assigned to the period under review. An example of an anticipated cost, that in connection with a warranty, has already been mentioned in this chapter, as well as examples of anticipated losses on bad debts and by fire. Losses similarly provided for in anticipation are those by flood, pilferage, and on investments.

Losses that can be allocated to specific assets, such as the loss on uncollectible receivables, are deducted in the balance sheet from the assets to which they apply. Those that cannot be allocated to specific assets are listed under the caption *Reserves* as seen in the balance sheet of the Leminto Corporation. The statements of this corporation show that as of June 30, 1964, the Reserve for warranty amounted to $52,780, of which $35,000 was added as of June 30, 1964, and that the Reserve for fire loss amounted to $18,640, of which $10,250 was added as of the close of the period. These reserves are listed under the head of liabilities although they are not items that require payment. They are, in fact, *contras* or deductions from the total assets. They are shown among the liabilities for want of a better place.

When a loss occurs, both the asset affected and its related reserve are reduced by the amount of the loss. If an anticipated loss, in whole or in part, does not occur, the amount provided is "restored to income," that is, it is added back, thus reversing the accounting procedure that created the reserve. All deductions from income for anticipated costs and losses are, accordingly, accounted for. The word *reserve* is used in a peculiar technical sense and it should not be regarded as signifying that something has been "set aside" or "saved up."

CORPORATE CAPITAL

The capital of a corporation consists of two elements: (1) capital stock, or basic investment of the stockholders, and (2) additional capital, or surplus, either contributed by the stockholders, accumulated through earnings, or acquired in other ways.

CAPITAL STOCK

Capital stock may have a *par value* or may be without par value. The par value of a share of stock is the amount of the investment, measured in terms of money, which an investor at the time of original issue must make in order to become the owner of a share of the stock. The par value is stated both in the corporation's charter and in the stock certificate.

There are several types of stock without par value that may be issued under the laws of the various states. The two important types are: (1) stock entirely without monetary designation that may be issued for such investment as is determined by the board of directors at the time of issue; (2) no-par stock with a *stated value* which sets a minimum investment to be received by the corporation upon issuance. The first type may be regarded as a "pure" no-par stock while the second is in the nature of a hybrid, partaking of the features of both par-value and no-par-value stock.

DIVIDENDS

Dividends constitute the income received by the stockholders on their investment in the corporation. They are paid only when the board of directors has taken formal action to *declare them*. When declared they become a current liability of the corporation.

CLASSES OF CAPITAL STOCK

The capital stock may be divided into various classes. The two main classes are: *common stock* and *preferred stock*.

As the name implies, the preferred stock has certain preferences. The forms of preference most commonly found are with respect to dividends and the division of assets in the event of liquidation of the corporation. When preferred stock has preference with respect to dividends, no dividends may be paid on the common stock unless the dividends are paid on the preferred stock. Preference in liquidation signifies that upon liquidation the preferred stockholders would be paid off before the common stockholders.

Preferred stock may be *cumulative* or *noncumulative*. If cumulative, any unpaid dividends or *dividends in arrears* accumulate until they are declared and paid; and no dividends may be paid on the common stock until all the accumulated or "passed" dividends on the preferred stock have been paid.

Dividends on preferred stock are limited to a certain rate but there is no limit to the dividends that may be paid on common stock. Dividends on par-value stock are declared as a certain percentage of par; on no-par-value stock they are declared as a certain sum per share.

Preferred stock may be *participating*. That is, it may participate with the common stock in any dividend paid on the common stock above a certain rate. To illustrate, let it be assumed that a certain corporation has issued a 6 per cent preferred stock that participates with the common stock in any dividend paid on the common stock above 8 per cent. Therefore, if at a certain time the dividend paid on the common stock should be one of 10 per cent, there would be paid the regular dividend of 6 per cent on the preferred stock plus an extra participating dividend of 2 per cent. It might be mentioned here that participating preferred stock has gone out of fashion.

The balance sheet describes the stock and states the number of shares authorized and issued. From the balance sheet of the Leminto Corporation it is seen that there has been issued 7% cumulative preferred stock having a par of $100 and common stock without par value but with a stated value of $5 per share.

LEGAL CAPITAL

The legal capital of a corporation depends on the incorporation statute of the state in which the corporation is organized. However, the following generalizations may be made: (1) if the stock has a par value the legal capital is the total par value of all stock issued; (2) if the stock is without par value but has a stated value per share the legal capital is the total stated value of the stock issued, plus such amounts as the board of directors may add thereto; (3) if the stock is without par value or stated value and there are no special provisions in the law, the legal capital is the total consideration received from the stockholders for the stock.

The balance sheet of the Leminto Corporation shows that the legal capital is $1,700,000, consisting of $200,000 for the preferred stock and $1,500,000 for the common stock. If the corporation is incorporated under the laws of the State of New York, the excess above the stated value of the common stock paid in by the stockholders may be added to the legal capital. As of June 30, 1964, the directors have not done so. This amount could be paid back to the stockholders as a "return of capital" which means that it would not represent income to them if so returned.

ADDITIONS TO CAPITAL

The legal capital of a corporation may not be reduced without appropriate legal action. The reason for this is that the legal capital must be held intact for the protection of creditors since the liability of the stockholders is limited to payment in full for their stock subscriptions and when this has been done they have no responsibility to creditors for debts of the corporation as is the case of an individual proprietor or partner. Accounting, in accordance with this rule of law, requires that the additions to the capital be not merged with the capital stock figure but shown separately. There are two categories of additions to capital: (1) retained earnings or earned surplus, and (2) other additions to capital generally referred to as *capital surplus*.

RETAINED EARNINGS

The item *retained earnings* or *earned surplus* indicates the amount of accumulated net income that has not been paid out to the stockholders as dividends.

CAPITAL SURPLUS

In contemporary balance sheets there is a tendency not to use the term *capital surplus* but rather to use more descriptive terms such as *capital in excess of par value* (or *stated value*), when stock has been issued at a figure above par or stated value, or, for example, *additional capital through donation* when the addition to capital has been by donation, a matter that will be described later, and so forth.

SURPLUS RESERVES

A portion of the retained earnings may be appropriated for a specific purpose and thus temporarily made unavailable for disbursement as dividends. The restriction of the dividends may be merely at the discretion of the board of directors or it may have a legal basis.

A restriction of the amount available for dividends may be made, for example, when the corporation is planning an extension of plant facilities and consequently the board of directors chooses to retain a sufficiently large portion of the corporation's wealth within the business for this purpose. When the plant extension has been completed and paid for, the restriction of dividends is no longer necessary, and so the reserve is eliminated by being added back to the retained earnings.

Sometimes a reserve representing a subdivision of the retained earnings is created because of a legal restriction on the retained earnings. This occurs when the corporation has borrowed money and has made an agreement with the lenders that a certain portion of its retained earnings shall not be available for dividends until the loan has been paid, or when a restriction has been placed on the retained earnings by a court as the result of litigation.

Surplus reserves are sometimes referred to as *appropriated surplus*, the remaining surplus being called *free surplus*.

Surplus reserves are shown in the balance sheet immediately after the free surplus and are added thereto since they are part of the surplus. The Leminto Corporation's balance sheet contains no surplus reserves.

It should be mentioned that the creation of surplus reserves tends to be discontinued. Instead, reasons for restriction of dividends are now shown in notes to the balance sheet. These notes comprise not only information regarding restrictions of the retained earnings but many other matters of interest to stockholders and others interested in the affairs of the business.

LEMINTO CORPORATION
RETAINED EARNINGS STATEMENT
FOR YEAR ENDED JUNE 30, 1964

Retained earnings, July 1, 1963		$ 57,545
Add Net income for the year		210,471
Adjustment of 1962-63 depreciation		125
		$268,141
Less Dividend on 7% preferred stock	$14,000	
Dividend on common stock,		
$.30 per share	88,500	102,500
Retained earnings,		
June 30, 1964		$165,641

TREASURY STOCK

Stock fully paid for and issued and later reacquired by the corporation is known as *treasury stock*, also called *reacquired shares*. The stock may be reacquired either through purchase by the corporation or through donation by stockholders. Treasury stock should not be confused with unissued stock which is sometimes erroneously referred to as treasury stock.

There are various reasons for the creation of treasury stock. A corporation may purchase its own stock in order to create a market demand or for other purposes such as resale to officers or employees. Stockholders may donate stock to the corporation in order to enable it to obtain funds that cannot be obtained in other ways. This is so because a corporation unable to sell its unissued stock at par may sell treasury stock below par since it was originally issued at par. However, instead of using this donation procedure, a corporation having only par-value stock would be likely to switch to no-par stock by obtaining an amendment of its charter. The no-par stock could then be sold at any price.

Purchases by a corporation of its own outstanding stock are limited under the laws of various states to the extent of its retained earnings or surplus available for dividends. This limitation has been imposed in order that the legal or stated capital of the corporation will not be reduced. The principle involved is that the amount of net assets represented by the legal capital may not be dissipated by the corporation but held intact in order to protect the creditors, as has already been stated. When stock has been purchased for the creation of treasury stock the amount available for dividends is restricted to the extent of the sum paid for the stock; that is, the remainder after deducting the amount paid for the stock measures the extent to which surplus is available for dividends.

Treasury stock is usually shown in the balance sheet as a deduction from the total of the capital stock and surplus, as in the balance sheet of the Leminto Corporation. It is usually carried at cost.

THE RETAINED EARNINGS STATEMENT

The retained earnings statement of the Leminto Corporation for year ended June 30, 1964 is shown on page 66. It begins with the amount of the retained earnings as of July 1, 1963 to which is added the net income for the year ended June 30, 1964 and an adjustment of the previous year's depreciation. Corrections of the net income of prior periods affect the retained earnings since the net income of these periods was added to the retained earnings. Then, after deducting the dividends declared during the year, the balance is the amount of retained earnings as of June 30, 1964. The retained earnings statement thus constitutes a reconciliation of the balance of retained earnings at the end of the accounting period with that at the beginning.

THE POSITION STATEMENT

An alternative form of balance sheet is illustrated on pages 68–71. This form is known as the *position statement* form. Any balance sheet may be called a position statement since it shows the position of the assets, the liabilities, and the capital as of a certain date. However, this form is so called because those who use it call it a position statement instead of a balance sheet.

The position statement form is arranged vertically, starting with the current assets from which are deducted the cur-

LEMINTO CORPORATION
POSITION STATEMENT
JUNE 30, 1964

CURRENT ASSETS:

Cash		$ 242,163
Marketable securities, at cost (market $120,075)		122,650
Accounts receivable	$180,794	
Less Estimated bad debts	3,616	177,178
Inventories:		
Materials (at the lower of LIFO cost or market)		102,793
Work in process (at cost)		30,540
Finished goods (at LIFO cost)		362,795
Prepaid expenses		9,716
Total current assets		$1,047,835

CURRENT LIABILITIES:

Accounts payable	$ 97,365	
Accrued expenses	15,271	
Dividends payable	102,500	
Federal income taxes payable	216,552	
Sinking fund payment due July 1, 1964	20,000	
Total current liabilities		451,688
Working capital		$ 596,147

68

PROPERTY, PLANT, AND EQUIPMENT:

Land			$562,000
Factory building	$1,327,546		
Less Depreciation	362,850	964,696	
Machinery and equipment	$ 104,682		
Less Depreciation	17,385	87,297	
Trucks	$ 12,460		
Less Depreciation	3,487	8,973	
Salesroom furniture	$ 13,370		
Less Depreciation	1,425	11,945	
General office furniture	$ 14,297		
Less Depreciation	845	13,452	
Total property, plant, and equipment			1,648,363

GOODWILL 1

DEFERRED CHARGES:

Bond discount	$ 4,800	
Organization expense	3,250	
Total deferred charges		8,050

OTHER ASSETS:

Accounts receivable (not current)	$ 6,000	
Miscellaneous advances and deposits	8,500	
Total other assets		14,500
Total assets, less current liabilities (carried forward)		$2,267,061

Total assets, less current liabilities (brought forward) .. $2,267,061

FUNDED DEBT:

First mortgage, 5-year, 6% sinking-fund bonds,
due July 1, 1967 .... $ 80,000
Less Sinking fund payment due July 1, 1964 (above) 20,000
                                                                   ─────────
                                                                     60,000
    Total funded debt ....
                                                                   $2,207,061

RESERVES:

Reserve for warranty .... $ 52,780
Reserve for fire loss 18,640
                                                                   ─────────
    Total reserves ....
                                                                     71,420
    Excess of assets over liabilities (stockholders' equity) $2,135,641

REPRESENTED BY:

7% cumulative preferred stock, par $100		
Authorized and issued, 2,000 shares		$ 200,000
Common stock, no par, stated value $5		
Authorized, 500,000 shares		
Issued, 300,000 shares		1,500,000
Total capital stock		$1,700,000
Retained earnings (restricted $30,000 because of purchase of		
stock for the treasury)		165,641
Capital in excess of stated value of common stock		300,000
		$2,165,641
Less Treasury stock—Common		
5,000 shares, at cost		30,000
		$2,135,641

rent liabilities to arrive at the *working capital*. This excess of the current assets over the current liabilities is often used as a measure of current position. It will be discussed at length in later chapters.

To the working capital are added the various noncurrent assets to produce the total of the assets less current liabilities. From this are deducted any other liabilities to arrive at the excess of assets over liabilities which, of course, is the amount of the stockholders' equity or capital.

Finally, there is shown the composition of the stockholders' equity.

THE SINGLE-STEP INCOME STATEMENT

The income statements previously illustrated are arranged in several steps, each followed by a subtotal. Because the various subtotals usually have little significance and are subject to misinterpretation, the form illustrated on page 73, in which all manner of income is placed in one group and all deductions from income in another, the total of which is deducted from the total income in one step, is known as the *single-step* income statement. It is used extensively in corporate reports to stockholders.

THE COMBINED INCOME AND RETAINED EARNINGS STATEMENT

Many corporations combine the income statement and the retained earnings statement into one, as shown in the single-step income statement on page 73. In this form, to the net income for the year there is added the retained earnings at the beginning of the year and other additions to retained earnings. Then there are deducted all decreases in retained earnings to arrive at the amount of retained earnings at the end of the year as shown in the balance sheet.

CONSOLIDATED STATEMENTS

When a corporation owns all or at least 51 per cent of the stock of another corporation, known as a controlling in-

LEMINTO CORPORATION
COMBINED INCOME AND RETAINED EARNINGS STATEMENT
FOR YEAR ENDED JUNE 30, 1964

INCOME:

Sales, less discounts, returns, and allowances		$2,262,066
Profit on sale of securities		1,280
Interest on investments		1,842
Income from sale of waste		2,517
Total income		$2,267,705

DEDUCTIONS FROM INCOME:

Cost of goods sold		$1,236,602
Selling, general, and administrative expenses		555,205
Interest expense		650
Amortization of bond discount		1,600
Provision for warranty		35,000
Provision for fire loss		10,250
Loss on sale of equipment		1,375
Federal income taxes		216,552
Total deductions from income		$2,057,234
Net income for the year		$ 210,471
Add Retained earnings, July 1, 1963		57,545
Adjustment of 1962–63 depreciation		125
		$ 268,141
Less Dividend on 7% preferred stock	$14,000	
Dividend on common stock, $.30 per share	88,500	102,500
Retained earnings, June 30, 1964		$ 165,641

terest, the owning corporation is called the parent company and the owned corporation a subsidiary company. Such ownership of capital stock of one or more other corporations is a common practice in the organization of modern business.

The parent company and each of its subsidiaries are legally independent entities. Each has its own accounting records and prepares its own financial statements. However, from a realistic point of view the parent and its subsidiaries consti- tute one organization. It is, therefore, more informative to those interested in the organization to have statements that show the income and the financial position of the organization as a whole. Such financial statements are usually prepared by accountants; they are called *consolidated statements*.

The process of consolidating the statements of the parent company and its subsidiaries into one set of statements includes such matters as the elimination of intercompany transactions—for example, the purchase of goods by one of the related companies from another. A transaction of this nature is reflected in an account payable in the books of the purchasing company and an account receivable in the books of the selling company. These items must be eliminated since from the point of view of the organization as a whole such transactions correspond to transactions between departments of a single company.

When a subsidiary company is not wholly owned by the parent company, part of the subsidiary's stock is owned by others who are regarded by the parent company as "outsiders." It is then said that the parent company's interest is the *majority interest*, because it constitutes the majority of the shares of capital stock, and that the interest of the other stockholders is the *minority interest*. Since the consolidated balance sheet is essentially a statement of the majority interest, the minority interest is shown therein as a liability. Consolidated statements differ very little from those of a single corporation.

7. The Accounting Processes

THIS CHAPTER is designed to review the accounting processes already discussed and to provide a deeper understanding of the nature of the data produced by them.

COSTS

A business enterprise is continually incurring costs in order to carry on operations. Business costs may be divided into three categories:

(1) the cost of the fixed assets;
(2) the cost of what is dealt in:
    (a) in a merchandising business, the cost of the merchandise purchased for resale;
    (b) in a manufacturing business, the cost of the materials, labor, and other costs to produce the products sold;
    (c) in a service business, the cost of the services performed; and
(3) the cost of the selling, general, and administrative activities.

These costs are incurred for the purpose of earning revenue. They are, therefore, deducted from the revenue they were instrumental in earning to arrive at the net income for a period of time such as a year. The costs considered applicable to a certain year are deducted from the revenue of that year. They are said to have expired and are classified as expenses.

Costs that are not deemed to have expired are classified as *assets*. Accordingly, the assets listed in a balance sheet, with the exception of cash and claims to cash such as receivables and investments in securities are *unexpired costs*. With but few exceptions, such as land on which a building is built, they will in the course of time expire and be assigned as deductions from revenue.

DISPOSITION OF COSTS

The process of disposing of costs or matching them with revenue affects the financial statements as follows:

The cost of the fixed assets. That portion of the cost of the fixed assets applicable to the period under review is designated as *depreciation* and is deducted from the revenue in the income statement. It is deducted from the cost of the assets in the balance sheet along with any previously accumulated depreciation. The difference between the cost of each fixed asset and the accumulated depreciation of that asset is the book value of the asset or its unexpired or unamortized cost.

The cost of what is dealt in. That portion of the cost of what was acquired or produced for sale and which has been sold appears in the income statement as *cost of goods sold* (also called *cost of sales*) and is deducted from the sales revenue. In a service business the cost of the service is deducted from the revenue in similar manner. The unsold merchandise of a merchandising business and the materials and finished goods on hand in a manufacturing business, as well as any work in process of production, are shown in the balance sheet as *inventory*.

Selling, general, and administrative costs. The cost of the selling, general, and administrative activities applicable to the period under review, or expired cost, is deducted from revenue in the income statement. Those costs not applicable to the period, or unexpired costs, are shown in the balance sheet as *prepaid expenses* or *deferred charges*. On the other hand, when *accrued expenses* are recognized they are listed as liabilities in the balance sheet and added to the expenses in the income statement.

COST AND VALUE

From the foregoing it is seen that accounting deals with *costs*. It does not deal with *values* in the commonly accepted sense of the word.

Value may be defined as a measurement in terms of money for a particular purpose and the value will usually be different for each purpose. Take, for example, a building. It would have a market value in the real estate market, a replacement value (the cost of constructing a building just like it), an assessed value for tax purposes, an accounting book value (the cost less accumulated depreciation), and if owned by a public utility it might be assigned a value in connection with rate-making. There is no such thing as real, true, or absolute value.

In every-day conversation the word *value* has the connotation of market value. The uninformed reader of a balance sheet will naturally so regard the stated amounts of the property, plant, and equipment. It is important to understand that these stated amounts are the unamortized portions of the costs of the assets.

The accountant does not give consideration to the market value of the property, plant, and equipment because a going concern, that is, one that intends to stay in business, does not in the normal course of events intend to sell them. It needs these assets to carry on its activities. So that information concerning what could be obtained from them is immaterial and irrelevant. As has been indicated, data regarding operations are usually of much greater importance in forming an opinion about a business than information regarding its investment in assets. If at any time, however, a business should desire to obtain the market value of its property, plant, and equipment, it can obtain this information from an appraiser.

CONVENTIONAL NATURE OF ACCOUNTING DATA

In scrutinizing the assets in a balance sheet one finds a combination of: (1) facts, (2) conventions, (3) postulates, and (4) judgment.

Cash, the first item, is a fact. It is the amount of money available for use.

The sum of the accounts and notes receivable is a fact for it indicates what is owing to the business by debtors. However, this sum is modified by an estimate of how much will be collected. This estimate requires judgment.

The inventory is stated on a conventional basis such as the lower of cost or market; and cost may be on the FIFO or the LIFO basis or on one of several other bases among the generally accepted procedures from which the accountant may make a selection.

The property, plant, and equipment are stated on the basis of cost less depreciation computed according to that conventional procedure which the accountant judges to be the most appropriate in the particular case.

A balance sheet is thus largely a statement of an accountant's opinion based on conventional procedures. If some other accountant had performed the work there might be differences in the figures. It follows that the income statement is also a statement of the accountant's opinion because the procedures reflected in the balance sheet also affect the figures found in the income statement. Both are the result of the process of separating the expired and unexpired costs.

The balance sheet purports to measure the assets, the liabilities, and the capital as of a certain date. The income statement purports to measure the income for a period of time. Because it is impossible to make these measurements in a precise manner, various conventional procedures, such as those described above, have been adopted.

THE POSTULATES

In order to implement the conventions, various assumptions, or postulates, have been adopted.

The permanency postulate. There is an underlying assumption with respect to the balance sheet to the effect that the enterprise for which the statement is prepared will continue in business. This is the natural assumption in the absence of information to the effect that the business is to be liquidated. If it were to be liquidated, for example, the book value of the fixed assets would no longer have significance and some assets, such as organization expense, would have to be discarded. Thus the figures at which the assets are stated are on what is known as the "going-concern basis" which is derived from the permanency postulate.

The realization postulate. Another assumption usually made, particularly in the sale of goods, is that the revenue is earned when the sale is consummated. From the logical point of view, especially in a manufacturing business, the revenue accrues during production. It is, however, usually inconvenient to record such accrual and so the realization postulate has been adopted as a matter of expediency.

The money postulate. In performing his work the accountant makes the tacit assumption that the purchasing power of money is constant. He does not differentiate among the dollars of various years in which the dollar had a different purchasing power. As far as accounting is concerned, a dollar is a dollar no matter whether the transaction it measures took place in 1929, 1939, 1949, or 1959. This is, of course, an assumption that is contrary to fact but one which the accountant makes in order to facilitate his work.

Because of price-level changes, this assumption or postulate has been the subject of considerable criticism both within and outside the accounting profession. But since no technique has been developed that will make a satisfactory adjustment of the figures, accountants continue the traditional attitude toward the matter.

The price-level problem is not new to those who use the financial statements. No alert businessman ever accepted the accountant's statements without what he calls a "grain of salt" in which he includes mental adjustments for the fluctuations in the purchasing power of money.

CONSISTENCY IN ACCOUNTING PROCEDURES

It is sometimes said that "the accountant can make it come out as he pleases" because, as has been shown, in performing his work he makes a selection of procedures from among various alternatives, each of which would give different results. It is true that the results for the first year of the operation of a business would depend to a considerable extent on the choices made. But the rules of accounting provide a sort of safety device after this for, having made his selection of procedures, the accountant is required to continue to follow them consistently. He may not usually switch to procedures other than those selected. In case he finds it necessary to make a procedural change he is required to describe it in his report and state the difference caused by the change. A good illustration of this is afforded by the switch made by many companies some years ago from the FIFO to the LIFO basis in the treatment of inventories.

The principle of consistency results in stability of the data produced and places the statements of successive years on a comparable basis. Accordingly, it does not matter which of the generally accepted procedures are used in accounting for a particular business as long as they are consistently applied from year to year.

THE EFFECT OF JUDGMENT

It has been shown that not only do the figures in the financial statements depend on the procedures selected but also on the accountant's judgment. The results of operations for a certain year are affected by the opinion of the accountant in such matters as income and expense to be accrued and deferred and on such estimates as the amount of receivables that will become uncollectible. However, these decisions usually result merely in differences in the earnings figures of two successive years. For example, most expenses deferred in one year will be included in the next year's record. And if the estimate of uncollectible receivables was too high in a certain year, other things being equal, the estimate for the next year will be lowered.

Therefore, the long-term view obtained from a review of statements of several successive years tends to eliminate not only procedural differences but also differences in judgment. It also removes the possibility of a wrong impression gained from the statement of a single year that might be distorted by unusual situations.

STATUS OF THE BALANCE SHEET

It has been said that the balance sheet shows the financial condition of a business. However, the use of the word "condition" is apt to be misleading because it has too broad a connotation. Its use gives the impression that the balance sheet shows all aspects of the relation of an enterprise to the business world about it. But this is not so. There are many factors affecting the condition of a business which are not shown in a balance sheet; for example, contracts, commitments, technical problems in an industry, market conditions, taxation, tariffs, the public's demand for commodities, and the ability of the management. The information contained in the balance sheet is restricted to the results of transactions, measured in terms of money, recorded in the accounting records. Therefore, rather than to say that the balance sheet is a statement of the financial *condition* of a business, it is more correct to say that it is a statement of the financial *position* of the accounting for that business.

As has already been stated, information of interest to the reader which is not contained in the accounting records and is, therefore, not in the financial statements is appended to them in the form of notes. These notes tend to bridge the gap between condition and financial position. It should be borne in mind that condition cannot be stated in definite dollars as can the accounting position.

In times past, accounting for the proprietary equity was regarded as the main objective of the accounting processes. Therefore, the balance sheet was regarded as the primary statement since it provided a measure of the proprietary equity. What was then called the profit and loss statement was regarded as a secondary statement that accounted for the change in the proprietary equity between balance-sheet dates. In more recent times, recognition has been given to the fact that earnings constitute a better measure of the satisfactoriness of a business than the amount of the investment therein. A business is organized to earn income and it cannot be regarded as successful if the income is not adequate no matter how great the investment in the business might be. As a result, the income statement is today regarded as the primary statement and the balance sheet a record of the residue of the assets and the equities therein carried forward for future operations. Because of the complementary nature of the statements, both are important to those interested in the business.

8. Comparative Statements

CHAPTERS 4 TO 7 have been devoted to an exposition of the form, the content, and the nature of the financial statements. Let us now proceed with a study of ways and means of interpreting their contents for the purpose of forming an opinion of the condition of a business. Although, as has been stated, the balance sheet does not by itself show such

ROBERT STOWELL
INCOME STATEMENT
FOR YEAR ENDED DECEMBER 31, 1962

INCOME:

Delivery charges	$131,425	
Rental charges	5,483	
Total income		$136,908

EXPENSES:

Gasoline and oil	$ 6,844
Wages	56,546
Payroll taxes	2,677
Truck maintenance and repairs	3,806
Rent	7,200
Heat and light	1,074
Insurance	1,825
Interest	395
Telephone	749
Supplies	4,560
Miscellaneous expense	3,543
Depreciation of trucks	6,120
Depreciation of furniture and equipment	435
Bad debts	110
Total expenses	95,884
Net income for the year	$ 41,024

condition, the data contained therein, together with those contained in the income statement, are useful as a basis for evaluating condition.

Valuable information is obtained by a comparison of the financial statements of a business from year to year. To facilitate such comparisons, *comparative statements* are prepared. For a demonstration of this, let us turn back to the case of Robert Stowell in Chapter 4. His income statement for year ended December 31, 1963 is shown on page 23 and his income statement for year ended December 31, 1962 is found on page 82. These two statements are combined into a *comparative income statement* on page 84. Note that there is provided in this statement a column in which are indicated the increases and decreases of the various items.

From Mr. Stowell's comparative income statement we learn that although his revenue, or income, during 1963 was $21,667 greater than in 1962, his net income was $1,302 less than in 1962. We further see that the reason for the decline in net income was an increase of $22,969 in the expenses. Scrutinizing the list of expenses, we find that the important increases were in wages, $10,962, depreciation of trucks, $4,225, truck maintenance and repairs, $2,356, and gasoline and oil, $1,401. It appears that because business activity increased, Mr. Stowell purchased additional trucks. This increased the depreciation for the year, the cost of truck maintenance and repairs, and the amount of gasoline and oil consumed. Also, in order to operate the additional trucks Mr. Stowell had to hire more help, thus increasing the amount of wages. We conclude from this that although Mr. Stowell did more business in 1963 than in 1962, it was less profitable because he had to increase his expenses at a higher rate than his income increased.

On pages 86–87 we find Mr. Stowell's balance sheet as of December 31, 1962 and on pages 88–89 a comparative balance sheet for his business as of December 31, 1962 and 1963. Here we see from the increase in trucks that Mr. Stowell's new trucks cost $20,200. We also see an increase in the accumulated depreciation of trucks of $10,345, the amount of the 1963 depreciation.

Further examination of the comparative balance sheet reveals several favorable features. Mr. Stowell's capital increased $9,722, apparently because he withdrew less than the amount of his net income. His cash on hand on December 31, 1963 was $2,576 greater than on December 31, 1962. In fact, the total of his assets increased $16,341, while his liabilities increased only $6,619, a favorable indi-

ROBERT STOWELL

COMPARATIVE INCOME STATEMENT

FOR YEARS ENDED DECEMBER 31, 1962 AND 1963

	1963	1962	Increase Decrease*
INCOME:			
Delivery charges	$152,367	$131,425	$20,942
Rental charges	6,208	5,483	725
Total income	$158,575	$136,908	$21,667
EXPENSES:			
Gasoline and oil	$ 8,245	$ 6,844	$ 1,401
Wages	67,508	56,546	10,962
Payroll taxes	3,350	2,677	673
Truck maintenance and repairs	6,162	3,806	2,356
Rent	7,200	7,200	
Heat and light	912	1,074	162*
Insurance	3,200	1,825	1,375
Interest	130	395	265*
Telephone	875	749	126
Supplies	6,221	4,560	1,661
Miscellaneous expense	3,690	3,543	147
Depreciation of trucks	10,345	6,120	4,225
Depreciation of furniture and equipment	862	435	427
Bad debts	153	110	43
Total expenses	$118,853	$ 95,884	$22,969
Net income for the year	$ 39,722	$ 41,024	$ 1,302*

cation. This type of analysis of changes from year to year is a horizontal analysis of comparative statements. It can be performed for any number of years to study the trends in a business.

Another kind of analysis that can be performed is that of proportions within one statement, a vertical study in one column of a comparative statement. For example, one of the proportions commonly studied is that of the relation of the current assets to the current liabilities. The current liabilities are those that the business will have to pay during the coming year. The amount of the current assets represents what the business has or will have available to pay these liabilities. On December 31, 1963, Mr. Stowell's current liabilities were $10,342 and his current assets $24,519. Of course, liabilities are paid in cash. But since these are undoubtedly not all payable immediately, receivables will probably be collected in time to pay those maturing in the future. To get an overall estimate of debt-paying ability we may measure the *current position* by the use of a *ratio*. Dividing the current assets, $24,519, by the current liabilities, $10,342, we obtain a ratio of about 2.4 to 1, indicating that for each dollar of current debts, Mr. Stowell has about $2.40 of assets, most of which will be converted into cash available to pay his debts. So we conclude that he will probably be able to meet his obligations.

Other relationships may also be studied. At the beginning of 1963, Mr. Stowell's capital was about $42,000. Since he earned about $40,000, we find by dividing $40,000 by $42,000 that his earnings were about 95 per cent on the investment, a handsome return. So we come up with the conclusion that although Mr. Stowell's earnings had declined from what they were the previous year, his business is eminently successful and that his debt-paying ability is very high. These are two important factors in the analysis of a business.

Another measure of liquidity is that of the dollars of *working capital*. The capital of a business is the excess of assets over liabilities. In similar manner, concentrating on the current sections of the balance sheet, we may calculate the excess of *current* assets over *current* liabilities. In the case of Robert Stowell, the working capital as of December 31, 1963 is obtained by deducting the current liabilities of $10,342 from the current assets of $24,519, making a working capital of $14,177.

The working capital of a business is theoretically the dollars of current assets against which there is no claim of

ROBERT STOWELL
BALANCE SHEET
DECEMBER 31, 1962

Assets

CURRENT ASSETS:

Cash			$ 4,296
Accounts receivable	$12,403		
Less Estimated bad debts	126		12,277
Prepaid expenses:			
Insurance	$ 1,280		
Supplies	928		2,208
Total current assets			$18,781

FIXED ASSETS:

Trucks	$30,500	
Less Accumulated depreciation	10,905	$19,595
Furniture and equipment	$10,872	
Less Accumulated depreciation	3,388	7,484
Total fixed assets		27,079
		$45,860

Liabilities and Capital

CURRENT LIABILITIES:

Accounts payable		$ 3,345
Accrued expenses:		
Wages	$ 350	
Interest	278	628
Total current liabilities		$ 3,973
ROBERT STOWELL, CAPITAL		41,887
		$45,860

87

ROBERT STOWELL
COMPARATIVE BALANCE SHEET
DECEMBER 31, 1962 AND 1963

Assets	1963	1962	Increase Decrease*
CURRENT ASSETS:			
Cash	$ 6,872	$ 4,296	$ 2,576
Accounts receivable	15,278	12,403	2,875
Accrued income:			
Delivery charges	385	—	385
Prepaid expenses:			
Insurance	1,250	1,280	30*
Interest	40	—	40
Supplies	863	928	65*
	$24,688	$18,907	$ 5,781
Less Estimated bad debts	169	126	43
Total current assets	$24,519	$18,781	$ 5,738

FIXED ASSETS:

Trucks	$50,700	$30,500	$20,200
Furniture and equipment	12,482	10,872	1,610
	$63,182	$41,372	$21,810
Less Accumulated depreciation:			
Trucks	$21,250	$10,905	$10,345
Furniture and equipment	4,250	3,388	862
	$25,500	$14,293	$11,207
Net fixed assets	$37,682	$27,079	$10,603
	$62,201	$45,860	$16,341

Liabilities and Capital

CURRENT LIABILITIES:

Notes payable	$ 3,500	$ —	$ 3,500
Accounts payable	6,247	3,345	2,902
Accrued expenses:			
Wages	575	350	125
Interest	20	278	258*
Total current liabilities	$10,342	$ 3,973	$ 6,369

DEFERRED INCOME:

Delivery charges	250	—	250
Total liabilities	$10,592	$ 3,973	$ 6,619
ROBERT STOWELL, CAPITAL	51,609	41,887	9,722
	$62,201	$45,860	$16,341

current creditors; and so it has been reasoned that it represents sums which the business may use as it pleases without concern about having funds available to pay debts. But here we have another problem in terminology. Economists refer to assets as "capital" and call current assets "working capital." When they deduct the current liabilities from the current assets, they call the difference the "net working capital." Therefore, when the term "working capital" is used, it is necessary to specify whether it is used in the accounting or economic sense. In this book it is used in the accounting sense.

From the foregoing it is seen that comparative statements may be analyzed both *horizontally* and *vertically*. This is the fundamental feature of financial statement analysis.

9. Analysis of Cash Flow

CASE NO. 1: ROBERT STOWELL

UPON EXAMINING the financial statements received from his accountant, as illustrated in Chapter 8, Robert Stowell exclaimed: "Although my income statement shows a net income for 1963 amounting to $39,722, my balance sheet shows that I had only $2,576 more cash at the end of the year than at the beginning. What became of all the money?" In response to this challenge the accountant proceeded to make an analysis of the flow of cash during the year and came up with the cash flow statement shown on pages 92–93.

It should be noted that this statement contains not only the effect of the operation of the business on the cash but also the receipt and disbursement of cash as the result of other activities. The statement presents a reconciliation, in summary form, of the cash on hand at the beginning and end of the year.

In order to produce a cash flow statement the accountant proceeds to convert the figures contained in the income statement from the accrual basis to the cash basis by the use of the data contained in the "increase-decrease" column of the comparative balance sheet, supplemented by an analysis of certain of the changes obtained from the accounting records. In the case of Robert Stowell the supplementary information was as follows:

The estimate of bad debts as of December 31, 1963 was $153. The balance sheet figure as of this date exceeds this amount by $16, the overestimate as of December 31, 1962. Therefore, the accounts receivable found uncollectible during 1963 must have amounted to $110, causing a loss of revenue to this extent. The accounting records show that the accounts involved were for delivery charges.

The increase in accounts receivable of $2,875 was for delivery charges.

The increase of $3,500 in notes payable was the result of a bank loan.

The increase in accounts payable was for the following:

ROBERT STOWELL
CASH FLOW STATEMENT
FOR YEAR ENDED DECEMBER 31, 1963

CASH WAS INCREASED BY OPERATIONS FROM:

Delivery charges	$149,247	
Rental charges	6,208	$155,455

CASH WAS DECREASED BY OPERATIONS FOR:

Gasoline and oil	$ 7,435	
Wages	67,283	
Payroll taxes	3,222	
Truck maintenance and repairs	6,162	
Rent	7,200	
Heat and light	756	
Insurance	3,170	
Telephone	850	
Supplies	5,873	
Miscellaneous expense	3,690	
Interest	428	106,069
Cash provided by operations		$ 49,386

CASH WAS INCREASED BY OTHER CAUSES:

Bank loan	3,500
	$ 52,886

CASH WAS DECREASED BY OTHER CAUSES:

Withdrawals by Mr. Stowell	$ 30,000	
Purchase of trucks	18,700	
Purchase of furniture and equipment	1,610	50,310
Increase in cash		$ 2,576

Gasoline and oil	$ 810
Payroll taxes	128
Heat and light	156
Telephone	25
Supplies	283
Purchase of trucks	1,500
	$2,902

ROBERT STOWELL
WORK SHEET FOR CASH FLOW STATEMENT
FOR YEAR ENDED DECEMBER 31, 1963

	Accrual Basis	Adjustments Add	Deduct	Cash Basis
Delivery charges	$152,367			
Not collected			$ 2,875	
Loss on uncollectibles			110	
Accrued but not collected			385	
Collected but deferred		$250		$149,247
Rental charges	6,208			6,208
	$158,575			$155,455
Gasoline and oil	$ 8,245			$7,435
Unpaid			810	
Wages	67,508			67,283
Accrued, not paid			225	
Payroll taxes	3,350			3,222
Unpaid			128	
Truck maintenance and repairs	6,162			6,162
Rent	7,200			7,200
Heat and light	912			756
Unpaid			156	
Insurance	3,200			3,170
Paid in prior period			30	
Telephone	875			850
Unpaid			25	

94

Supplies 6,221   283 ....
  Unpaid 5,873
  Paid in prior period 3,690
Miscellaneous expense 3,690   65 ....
Interest 130
  Paid in advance 40
  Accrued in prior period; paid in this period 258   428
Depreciation of trucks 10,345   10,345 ....
  Did not require disbursement of cash .... —
Depreciation of furniture and equipment 862   862 ....
  Did not require disbursement of cash .... —
Bad debts 153   153 ....
  Did not require disbursement of cash .... —

                               $118,853 $106,069

Net income for the year (accrual basis) .... $ 39,722 $ 49,386

   Cash provided by operations ....

Add cash received from:
  Bank loan 3,500
                                    $ 52,886

Deduct cash disbursed for:
  Withdrawals by Mr. Stowell .... $ 20,200 $ 30,000
  Purchase of trucks 18,700
    Unpaid 1,500   1,610
  Purchase of furniture and equipment .... $ 50,310

     Increase in cash .... $ 2,576

95

Mr. Stowell withdrew $30,000 for personal use.

The principle involved in the preparation of the cash flow statement is shown in the work sheet on pages 94–95. The professional accountant would not prepare his work sheet in the manner illustrated; the arrangement here used is for the purpose of making it understandable to the non-accountant.*

From an examination of the work sheet it is seen that from the delivery charges as reported on the accrual basis there is deducted the amount of the increase in accounts receivable which indicates the sum not collected. There is also deducted the loss on uncollectible accounts and the amount of accrued delivery income included on the accrual basis but not collected. On the other hand, there is added the $250 collected but deferred on the accrual basis.

Adjustments of the expenses are:

Prepaid expenses. Insurance and supplies are reduced, respectively $30 and $65, for the decrease in the amounts prepaid in prior period but included in the 1963 income statement on the accrual basis. Interest expense, $40, was deferred and so not included in the 1963 expense on the accrual basis, but since it was paid in 1963 this amount is added to the interest expense on the cash basis.

Accrued expenses. Included in the wages on the accrual basis was $225 wages accrued. Since this was not paid in 1963 it is deducted in conversion to the cash basis. In 1962, $258 interest was included on the accrual basis but the decrease in the comparative balance sheet of this amount indicates that it was paid in 1963. It is therefore added in converting to the cash basis.

Accounts payable. The increases in accounts payable for various expenses indicate nonpayment of the sums indicated. Therefore, they have been deducted from the expenses in conversion to the cash basis. The amount unpaid on the purchase of trucks has been deducted from the purchase price.

Because depreciation and bad debts are items not requiring disbursement of cash, they are deducted in converting to the cash basis.

---

* For an exposition of the professional procedure see John N. Myer, *Financial Statement Analysis*, pages 115-126. Englewood Cliffs, N. J.: Prentice-Hall, Inc., 3d edition, 1961.

CASE NO. 2: SAM GOODWIN

Let us now consider the case of Sam Goodwin who operates a merchandising business and whose income statement for year ended December 31, 1963, in condensed form, that is, with certain details omitted, is found on page 98. The following additional information regarding 1963 operations has been obtained from the accounting records: Furniture which had cost $890 and had been depreciated $620, so that the unamortized cost was $270, was sold for $150, with a loss of unamortized cost of $120. Accounts receivable written off amounted to $299. Furniture and fixtures were purchased for $8,250. Mr. Goodwin withdrew $20,000.

The work sheet for the preparation of Mr. Goodwin's cash flow statement for year ended December 31, 1963 is shown on pages 99–100. The important difference between this work sheet and that for the business of Robert Stowell is the derivation of the amount of cash paid for merchandise purchased from the cost of goods sold on the accrual basis.

The cost of goods sold section of the income statement can be constructed from the information available as follows:

Inventory, January 1	$15,920
Add Purchases	69,965
	$85,885
Less Inventory, December 31	22,426
Cost of goods sold	$63,459

SAM GOODWIN
INCOME STATEMENT
FOR YEAR ENDED DECEMBER 31, 1963

Sales (net)		$122,860
Less:		
Cost of goods sold	$63,459	
Selling, general, and administrative expenses	28,843	
Depreciation	1,875	
Provision for bad debts	450	
Loss on sale of furniture	120	94,747
Net income for the year		$ 28,113

The balances of various accounts were:

| | December 31 | | Increase |
	1963	1962	Decrease*
Cash	$ 6,572	$ 9,036	$2,464*
Accounts receivable (customers)	10,874	12,596	1,722*
Merchandise inventory	22,426	15,920	6,506
Accounts payable (merchandise purchases)	8,726	4,245	4,481
Accounts payable (expenses)	1,372	6,193	4,821*
Prepaid expenses	685	782	97*
Accrued expenses	1,456	1,052	404

SAM GOODWIN

WORK SHEET FOR CASH FLOW STATEMENT
FOR YEAR ENDED DECEMBER 31, 1963

	Accrual Basis	Adjustments Add	Adjustments Deduct	Cash Basis
Sales (net)	$122,860			
Collections in excess of year's sales		$1,722		
Accounts written off			$ 299	$124,283
	$122,860			$124,283
Cost of goods sold	$ 63,459			
Excess of final over initial inventory		6,506		
Merchandise not paid for			4,481	
Payments for merchandise purchases				$ 65,484
Selling, general, and administrative expenses	28,843			
Expenses of 1962 paid for in 1963		4,821		
Expenses of 1963 paid for in 1962		97		
Unpaid			404	33,163.

99

Depreciation 1,875
  Did not require disbursement of cash .... 1,875 .... —

Provision for bad debts 450
  Did not require disbursement of cash .... 450 .... —

Loss on sale of furniture 120
  Did not require disbursement of cash .... 120 .... —

                                                   $ 94,747 .... $ 98,647

Net income for the year .... $ 28,113

Cash provided by operations .... $ 25,636

Add cash received from:
Sale of furniture 150
                                      $ 25,786

Deduct cash disbursed for:
Purchase of furniture and fixtures .... $ 8,250
Withdrawals by Mr. Goodwin 20,000
                                      $ 28,250

Decrease in cash .... $ 2,464

SAM GOODWIN
CASH FLOW STATEMENT
FOR YEAR ENDED DECEMBER 31, 1963

CASH WAS INCREASED BY OPERATIONS FROM:

Sales $124,283

CASH WAS DECREASED BY OPERATIONS FOR:

Purchase of merchandise	$65,484	
Selling, general, and administrative expenses	33,163	98,647
Cash provided by operations		$ 25,636

CASH WAS INCREASED BY OTHER CAUSES:

Sale of furniture 150

$ 25,786

CASH WAS DECREASED BY OTHER CAUSES:

Purchase of furniture and fixtures	$ 8,250	
Withdrawals by Mr. Goodwin	20,000	28,250
Decrease in cash		$ 2,464

The cost of the merchandise purchased is obtained by adding to the cost of goods sold, $63,459, the December 31 inventory, $22,426, and deducting the January 1 inventory, $15,920. The same result is obtained by adding the excess of the December 31 inventory over the January 1 inventory, $6,506, to the cost of goods sold. Since there was an increase of $4,481 in the accounts payable for merchandise purchases, indicating the amount of purchases not paid for, the cash disbursed for merchandise purchased during the year was $65,484.

The decrease in accounts payable for expenses of $4,821 indicates that the equivalent of the accounts payable for expenses of 1963 were paid for, plus 1962 expenses amounting to $4,821.

The other adjustments are similar to those in the work sheet for the business of Robert Stowell.

The cash flow statement for the business of Sam Goodwin for year ended December 31, 1963 is shown on page 101.

CASE NO. 3: BOLANDO CORPORATION

The Bolando Corporation is a manufacturing enterprise. The work sheet for conversion of its income statement for year ended December 31, 1963 into a cash flow statement is found on pages 104–5. For simplicity, the three inventories—materials, work in process, and finished goods—are treated as one inventory. The reader should now have no difficulty in understanding the conversion process, although there are more items in this case than in the previous ones. Note the elimination of depreciation, amortization, loss of unamortized cost of machinery, and estimated provisions since these do not require disbursement of cash. The cash flow statement of the Bolando Corporation for year ended December 31, 1963 is indicated in the last column of the work sheet.

THE CONVERSION PROCESS

It will have been observed that the process of conversion of the *net income for the year* (on the accrual basis) to *cash provided by operations* consists of undoing the work of the accrual basis of allocating revenue to periods of time and then matching with it the costs that are judged to have been and will be incurred in earning that revenue. This is necessary because some of the movement of cash does not take place in the same period in which the corresponding revenues and costs are given recognition in accrual accounting. For example, in the cash flow statement the item *sales* may include cash received from sales made the previous year, the year under review, and some that will be consummated the following year. In similar manner, the cash paid for expenses may include some of the expenses of the previous year, the year under review, and some of the next year.

The conversion process, as has been seen, requires adjustments for the changes in receivables, payables, accrued and deferred income and expense, and the non-cash items such as amortizations, estimated provisions, and gains and losses on certain purchases and sales.

FUNCTION OF CASH FLOW STATEMENT

The income statement provides a report on the results of operations during a certain period: it measures the revenue and the cost of achieving it. The balance sheet measures the assets carried forward into the next period and the equities in those assets. These measurements are in terms of money, the common denominator of all accounting.

The principal movement of capital (used in the economic sense and in a simplified manner) is from cash to physical assets, such as plant, equipment, and inventory, then to receivables, and finally back to cash which is disbursed for various purposes. In the case of the Bolando Corporation we see that in 1963 cash flowed into the business not only as the result of operations but also through equity financing (sale of capital stock) and incidentally from compensation received from an insurance company and the sale of land, machinery, equipment, and marketable securities. The cash then flowed into the form of buildings, equipment, and inventories. The inventories, as a result of product sales, flowed into the form of receivables which were then converted back to cash. The cash flowed out for debt retirement, payment of dividends and warranty claims, purchase of securities, and payment of operating costs. Cash is the life-blood of a business. The operating cycle begins and ends with cash.

Because of the importance of cash, management is deeply concerned with the control of its flow into and out of the business and needs to see to it that an adequate supply is

BOLANDO CORPORATION
WORK SHEET FOR CASH FLOW STATEMENT
FOR YEAR ENDED DECEMBER 31, 1963

	Income Statement	Adjustments Add	Adjustments Deduct	Cash Flow Statement
Sales (net)	$4,065,365			
Increase in accounts receivable			$ 55,243	$4,007,257
Write-offs of accounts receivable			2,865	
Interest on investments	5,075			5,075
Profit on sale of marketable securities	1,928		1,928	
Profit on sale of land	25,600		25,600	
	$4,097,968			$4,012,332
Cost of goods sold	$2,062,540			
Increase in inventories		$64,514		
Decrease in accounts payable (trade)		17,619		
Cost of raw materials and other manufacturing costs paid for				$2,144,673
Selling, general, and administrative expenses	1,582,768			
Increase in prepaid expenses		2,109		
Increase in accrued expenses			6,426	1,578,451
Depreciation of buildings	92,587		92,587	—
Depreciation of machinery and equipment	106,270		106,270	—
Amortization of patents	2,500		2,500	—
Amortization of bond discount	1,500		1,500	—
Taxes (other than income taxes)	38,762			38,762
Provision for warranty	8,245		8,245	—

Provision for bad debts	3,500	
Interest on bonds	10,625	10,625
Other interest	962	962
Loss on sale of machinery	1,246	
Provision for federal income taxes	82,138	82,138
	$3,993,643	$3,773,473
Net income for the year	$ 104,325	
Cash provided by operations		$ 238,859
Add cash received from:		
Sale of land		200,000
Sale of machinery and equipment		2,500
Compensation received from insurance company		25,350
Sale of capital stock		500,000
Sale of marketable securities		12,755
		$ 979,464
Deduct cash disbursed for:		
Additions to buildings		$ 205,390
Purchase of machinery and equipment		98,353
Payment of warranty claims		5,629
Redemption of debentures		50,000
Purchase of marketable securities		26,250
Payment of dividends		200,000
Payment of 1962 federal income taxes		78,340
		$ 663,962
Increase in cash		$ 315,502

available at all times. Therefore, a report that relates the flow of cash to operations is important to management. The cash flow statement shows how the activities reported on in the income statement were financed. It also summarizes the financial transactions that caused changes in the assets, the liabilities, and the capital as shown in the related balance sheet. The cash flow statement is also useful as a basis for budgeting and other planning for the future since hindsight may well be used as a starting point for foresight. Accordingly, the cash flow statement, relatively a newcomer, should, in the opinion of many accountants, be made a part of regular accounting procedure.

The cash flow statement as here outlined can usually be produced only once a year and, as in the case of the other financial statements, is historical in nature. Since control of cash is constantly necessary, management requires frequent data on the cash position and this can be made available by the accountant monthly, weekly, and even daily. However, such reports are outside the scope of the present book.

CASH FLOW AND DEPRECIATION

It is sometimes said that the "cash flow" figure—referring to what is here called *cash provided by operations*—may be defined as net income plus depreciation. The reader will readily realize from the foregoing exposition that this is quite incorrect because in the conversion process there are matters involved other than depreciation.

However, in the case of a large industrial enterprise where the depreciation is a relatively large figure, this item may well constitute the greater portion of the difference between the net income and the cash provided by operations. In fact, in certain cases the other items might be negligible. Therefore, in such case a rough estimate may be made by ignoring the other items. But instead of saying that the "cash flow" item consists of net income plus depreciation, it should be said that it is *net income without a deduction for depreciation*.

It might be argued that this is merely a play on words since the same figure will be obtained whether depreciation is added to the net income or whether the deduction for depreciation is eliminated from the net income figure. However, the notion that the cash provided by operations consists of net income plus depreciation leads to the erroneous conclusion to the effect that there are two sources of cash:

CASH FLOW STATEMENT

BALANCE, JANUARY 1		**$ 3,065,000**
SOURCES OF CASH:		
Net income	$ 2,780,000	
Short term bonds	10,000,000	
Depreciation	875,000	13,655,000
		$16,720,000
USES OF CASH:		
Increase in inventories	$ 5,025,000	
Increase in receivables and other current assets	1,762,000	
Decrease in accounts payable and other current liabilities	2,658,000	
Dividends	3,500,000	
Redemption of bonds	1,800,000	
Other, net	65,000	14,810,000
BALANCE, DECEMBER 31		**$ 1,910,000**

net income and depreciation, a fallacy which pervades much of economic and financial literature. To consider depreciation a source of cash is paradoxical. Depreciation is the cost of fixed assets that has been assigned to the period under review—a cost, not a gain.

As a result of this erroneous concept one sometimes hears such statements as that a certain corporation is obtaining sufficient cash from depreciation to finance its expansion plans. This, of course, is nonsense. If it were true, it would follow that cash is obtained from the other non-cash deductions from revenue, such as provisions for bad debts and fire loss, the amortization of bond discount and patents, and losses on sale of fixed assets.

ALTERNATIVE FORM OF THE CASH FLOW STATEMENT

Some corporations, in their reports to stockholders, use an arrangement of the cash flow statement such as that shown above. This arrangement unfortunately gives the impression that depreciation is a source of cash. The statement also loses its effectiveness by combining sales, cost of goods sold, and operating expenses into one figure, net income. Also, the adjustments to the cash basis are shown in two figures: changes in "receivables and other current assets," and changes in "accounts payable and other current liabilities." Although this statement achieves a reconciliation of the cash balances at the beginning and end of the period, it does not provide properly adjusted information with respect to the flow of cash.

In order to overcome the erroneous impression that depreciation is a source of cash, some corporations using the foregoing form treat depreciation as follows:

SOURCES OF CASH:

Net income	$ 2,780,000	
Add Depreciation which required no disbursement of cash	875,000	
	$ 3,655,000	
Short term bonds	10,000,000	$13,655,000

MISUSE OF THE "CASH FLOW" FIGURE

The "cash provided by operations" is really the difference between the cash provided and the cash applied to different uses. It is the net provision or net increase in cash by operations during the period.

This net increase in cash by operations, popularly designated the "cash flow," is sometimes used in unwarranted ways. For example, one may find in a corporation president's letter to the stockholders a statement such as that the net income for the year was $3,658,000 but that the cash flow was $4,875,000, thus suggesting that the "real" earnings were greater than is shown by the accountant's income statement.

The cash flow statement takes a narrow point of view. Its scope is limited to a summary of the cash transactions during a period, disregarding events that have occurred in prior periods or will occur in future periods but which have a bearing on the operations of the period under review. Particularly is this true with respect to depreciation. A great amount of cash might have been spent in prior periods to make the operations of the period under review possible but it is not given recognition in the cash flow statement for the period. The income statement on the accrual basis takes a comprehensive view and thus provides the only satisfactory measure of the success of operations. It is conceivable that in a particular case business might have been very poor during a certain year but that nevertheless there was a large inflow of cash as the result of operations of the previous year. It is very misleading to compare the merits of the cash flow statement with those of the income statement. They are not comparable. The two statements serve different purposes.

ANALYSIS OF WORKING CAPITAL FLOW

Another kind of analysis sometimes made is that of the flow of working capital. As has already been explained, the working capital of a business, from the accounting point of view, is the excess of its current assets over its current liabilities. Although a business could conceivably have an excess of current liabilities over current assets, this condition is unusual and might indicate insolvency. A business having such excess of current liabilities over current assets would be said to have no working capital.

The executive desires to have an explanation of the changes that occurred in the current assets and current liabilities during a year. Such information is found in the comparative balance sheet and may be arranged in the form of a comparative working capital statement such as that illustrated on page 110, which has been prepared for the business of Sam Goodwin, our Case No. 2, as of December 31, 1962 and 1963.

This information, however, is insufficient. The executive desires to know what transactions took place to cause the changes in the current assets and current liabilities. In order to provide this information, we may prepare the work sheet shown on page 111. This work sheet does not require the detailed information from the accounting records such as an analysis of the receivables, payables, and the accrued and deferred income and expenses as is necessary for the preparation of the cash flow work sheet. Therefore, the working capital flow statement can be prepared for a business from its financial statements without access to the accounting records and so may even be prepared outside the business.

Note that the provision for bad debts is not eliminated, as it is from the cash flow statement, since the allowance for

SAM GOODWIN
COMPARATIVE WORKING CAPITAL STATEMENT
DECEMBER 31, 1962 AND 1963

	December 31 1963	December 31 1962	Working Capital Increase	Working Capital Decrease
CURRENT ASSETS:				
Cash	$ 6,572	$ 9,036		$ 2,464
Accounts receivable, less estimated bad debts	10,405	12,278		1,873
Merchandise inventory	22,426	15,920	$ 6,506	
Prepaid expenses	685	782		97
Total current assets	$40,088	$38,016		
CURRENT LIABILITIES:				
Accounts payable—merchandise	$ 8,726	$ 4,245		4,481
Accounts payable—expenses	1,372	6,193	4,821	
Accrued expenses	1,456	1,052		404
Total current liabilities	$11,554	$11,490		
Working capital	$28,534	$26,526	$11,327	$ 9,319
Increase in working capital				2,008
			$11,327	$11,327

SAM GOODWIN

WORK SHEET FOR WORKING CAPITAL FLOW STATEMENT
FOR YEAR ENDED DECEMBER 31, 1963

	Income Statement	Adjustments Add	Adjustments Deduct	Working Capital Flow Statement
Sales (net)	$122,860			$122,860
Cost of goods sold	$ 63,459			$ 63,459
Selling, general, and administrative expenses	28,843			28,843
Depreciation	1,875		$1,875	—
Provision for bad debts	450			450
Loss on sale of furniture	120		120	—
	$ 94,747			$ 92,752
Net income for the year	$ 28,113			
Working capital provided by operations				$ 30,108
Add increase in working capital from:				
Sale of furniture				150
				$ 30,258
Deduct decrease in working capital by:				
Purchase of furniture and fixtures				$ 8,250
Withdrawals by Mr. Goodwin				20,000
				$ 28,250
Increase in working capital				$ 2,008

SAM GOODWIN

WORKING CAPITAL FLOW STATEMENT

FOR YEAR ENDED DECEMBER 31, 1963

WORKING CAPITAL WAS INCREASED BY OPERATIONS FROM:

Sales (net)	$122,860

WORKING CAPITAL WAS DECREASED BY OPERATIONS FOR:

Cost of goods sold	$63,459	
Selling, general, and administrative expenses	28,843	
Provision for bad debts	450	92,752
Working capital provided by operations		$ 30,108

WORKING CAPITAL WAS INCREASED BY OTHER CAUSES:

Sale of furniture	150
	$ 30,258

WORKING CAPITAL WAS DECREASED BY OTHER CAUSES:

Purchase of furniture and fixtures	$ 8,250	
Withdrawals by Mr. Goodwin	20,000	28,250
Increase in working capital		$ 2,008

SAM GOODWIN

WORKING CAPITAL FLOW STATEMENT
FOR YEAR ENDED DECEMBER 31, 1963

WORKING CAPITAL WAS INCREASED BY OPERATIONS:

Net income for the year		$28,113
Add Deductions from revenue not affecting working capital:		
Depreciation	$ 1,875	
Loss on sale of furniture	120	1,995
		$30,108

WORKING CAPITAL WAS INCREASED BY OTHER CAUSES:

Sale of furniture		150
		$30,258

WORKING CAPITAL WAS DECREASED BY OTHER CAUSES:

Purchase of furniture and fixtures	$ 8,250	
Withdrawals by Mr. Goodwin	20,000	28,250
Increase in working capital		$ 2,008

bad debts is part of the working capital, a deduction from the receivables.

The working capital flow statement for the business of Sam Goodwin for year ended December 31, 1963, prepared from the work sheet, is shown on page 112. An alternative form of this statement, similar to the alternative form of the cash flow statement, and with similar shortcomings, is found on page 113.

Statements of the type here discussed are generally called *funds statements*. However, when the term "funds" is used, it is not clear whether the statement is on the cash or the working capital basis. It is preferable to avoid the use of the word "funds" and to indicate in the title of the statement the basis used.

10. Measurement of Changes

RATES OF CHANGE

IT WAS DEMONSTRATED in Chapter 8 how the statements of successive years may be compared by the use of comparative statements in which a column is provided to indicate the increases and decreases in the various items. In addition to the *absolute changes*, in dollars, the *rates of change* may be indicated by percentages. These are obtained by dividing the amount of the increase or decrease of an item by the amount of that item in the first of the years compared.

From the comparative income statement of the business of Arthur Milford for years ended December 31, 1962 and 1963 shown on page 116, it is seen that the sales in 1963 decreased $139,427 from those of 1962. Dividing $139,427 by $702,681, the 1962 sales, it is seen that the decrease was one of 19.8 per cent. The rate of change enables the reader of the statement to form an opinion with respect to the importance of the change. In the case of Mr. Milford, the decrease of $139,427 would be less serious if it were one of 5 per cent and more serious if it were one of 30 per cent.

Further scrutiny of the statement reveals that although Mr. Milford's sales decreased 19.8 per cent, his net income for the year increased 12.9 per cent. Between these percentages there is found the reason for the increase in net income in spite of the decrease in sales. There was a decrease of 27.8 per cent in the cost of goods sold and a decrease in total expenses of 1.2 per cent. The decrease in sales was more than offset by the decrease in cost of goods sold and expenses. The use of percentages simplifies comparison by relieving the mind of the relatively large dollar amounts.

ARTHUR MILFORD
COMPARATIVE INCOME STATEMENT
FOR YEARS ENDED DECEMBER 31, 1962 AND 1963

	1963	1962	Increase–Decrease* Amount	Per Cent
Sales (net)	$563,254	$702,681	$139,427*	19.8*
Cost of goods sold	367,162	508,320	141,158*	27.8*
Gross margin	$196,092	$194,361	$ 1,731	.9
Selling expenses	$107,296	$111,335	$ 4,039*	3.6*
General and administrative expenses	56,132	54,085	2,047	3.8
Total expenses	$163,428	$165,420	$ 1,992*	1.2*
Net income for the year	$ 32,664	$ 28,941	$ 3,723	12.9

Percentages of increase and decrease may also be applied to the comparative balance sheet as shown in the comparative balance sheet of Arthur Milford as of December 31, 1962 and 1963 on page 118. It is seen, for example, that Mr. Milford's current assets increased 9.0 per cent, while his current liabilities increased 20.0 per cent, an important point of information because the greater increase in current liabilities than in current assets tends to make his current position, or debt-paying ability, less favorable. The increase of 34.8 per cent in furniture and fixtures attracts attention. It may readily be expected that this increase in fixed assets, together with the increase in merchandise inventory of 3.4 per cent, caused the increase in current liabilities.

It should be noted that no rate of change can be indicated for an item when in the first of the years compared its amount is zero because if a number is divided by zero the quotient is infinity. This is seen in the case of the miscellaneous receivables in the comparative balance sheet of Arthur Milford.

In interpreting financial statements it is important to bear in mind that both the absolute change and the rate of change should be observed. For example, in the case under consideration, the prepaid expenses decreased 8.3 per cent. The decline, however, was one of only $114. Percentages tend to give an exaggerated impression of changes when the base is small.

COMMON-SIZE INCOME STATEMENT

As stated in Chapter 8, measurements may be made of the relationships within one statement. This constitutes a vertical study within one column of the comparative statement. It may be done in the form of what is known as a *common-size income statement* in which net sales is taken as the base, or 100 per cent, and each of the other items divided by the amount of net sales. The comparative common-size income statement for the business of Arthur Milford for years ended December 31, 1962 and 1963, page 119, shows that in 1963 the cost of goods sold was 65.2 per cent of net sales and the selling expenses 19.0 per cent.

A practical interpretation of this statement is to consider it as showing the distribution of the average sales dollar. Thus in 1963, 65.2 cents of each average dollar earned as

ARTHUR MILFORD
COMPARATIVE BALANCE SHEET
DECEMBER 31, 1962 AND 1963

Assets	1963	1962	Increase—Decrease* Amount	Increase—Decrease* Per Cent
Cash	$ 15,584	$ 17,132	$ 1,548*	9.0*
Accounts receivable (less estimated bad debts)	152,283	130,358	21,925	16.8
Merchandise inventory	126,763	122,602	4,161	3.4
Prepaid expenses	1,254	1,368	114*	8.3*
Total current assets	$295,884	$271,460	$24,424	9.0
Furniture and fixtures (less depreciation)	$ 40,528	$ 30,061	$10,467	34.8
Miscellaneous receivables	654	—	654	—
Total noncurrent assets	$ 41,182	$ 30,061	$11,121	37.0
	$337,066	$301,521	$35,545	11.8
Liabilities and Capital				
Notes payable (bank)	$ 60,000	$ 50,000	$10,000	20.0
Accounts payable	112,205	91,995	20,210	22.0
Accrued expenses	1,432	2,761	1,329*	48.1*
Total current liabilities	$173,637	$144,756	$28,881	20.0
Arthur Milford, Capital	$163,429	$156,765	$ 6,664	4.3
	$337,066	$301,521	$35,545	11.8

ARTHUR MILFORD
COMPARATIVE COMMON-SIZE INCOME STATEMENT
FOR YEARS ENDED DECEMBER 31, 1962 AND 1963

	1963	1962
Sales (net)	100.0%	100.0%
Cost of goods sold	65.2	72.3
Gross margin	34.8%	27.7%
Selling expenses	19.0%	15.9%
General and administrative expenses	10.0	7.7
Total expenses	29.0%	23.6%
Net income for the year	5.8%	4.1%

the result of sales was used to pay for the goods sold, 19.0 cents for selling expenses, and 10.0 cents for general and administrative expenses, leaving 5.8 cents of each dollar for the owner of the business.

By reading the statement horizontally comparison can be made of the operations of successive years. It is seen that in 1962, 72.3 cents of each average dollar was paid for the goods sold and that the cost was reduced to 65.2 cents in 1963; that in 1962, 15.9 cents of each average dollar was paid for selling expenses and that this rose to 19.0 cents in 1963. And so forth.

Because the total of the distribution of the parts of the average sales dollar to the various factors involved always equals 100 per cent, all statements in this form will total 100 per cent and so will be of a common size; hence the name given to the statement.

The comparative common-size income statement provides a starting point for operations analysis. The figures in the statement are the result of countless transactions, information concerning which is available in the accounting records. The executive may obtain such information from the accountant.

In a merchandising business, various reasons can be found for variation in the purchase prices. An increase in the rate of cost of goods sold may be the result of a rise in the price level or it may be due to inefficiency in purchasing. But whatever the cause may be, it can be determined and an effort can be made to remedy the situation. If in such a case the cost cannot be reduced, consideration should be given to increasing the selling price. Or, perhaps, both cost reduction and price increase can be effected. In a manufacturing business the matter is more complicated. This will be discussed in Chapter 15 on cost-volume-profit analysis.

COMPARATIVE EXPENSE SCHEDULES

The accountant can make available to the executive detailed schedules of the various operating expenses. Take, for example, the comparative schedule of selling expenses of the business of Arthur Milford for years ended December 31, 1962 and 1963 on page 121. From this schedule it is seen that although net sales decreased 19.8 per cent, salesmen's salaries increased 2.8 per cent. The reason for this increase can be obtained from the accounting and other records. It might be found that it was not possible to decrease the sales force and perhaps salaries had to be increased in line with the rise in the cost of living. It is also seen that in 1962, 8.0 cents of each average sales dollar was paid for salesmen's salaries, while in 1963, 10.3 cents was paid. This is to be expected because of the decline in sales and the rise in salesmen's salaries.

Although delivery expense usually correlates with sales, in 1962 it required 2.1 cents of the average sales dollar but in 1963 it increased to 2.5 cents in spite of the decline in sales. The reason could be obtained from the records. Depreciation, of course, increased because of the acquisition of additional fixed assets.

The cost of advertising does not necessarily correlate with the movement of sales. The decrease from 4.1 cents to 3.8 cents of the average sales dollar may have been due to the fact that in 1962 an unusual promotional effort was made. Or perhaps the decline was in the interest of economy. Details can be obtained.

It is thus seen that the executive will work backwards from the statements to the multifarious details that can be supplied by the accountant from the accounting records. This theme will be elaborated upon in the following chapters.

ARTHUR MILFORD

COMPARATIVE SCHEDULE OF SELLING EXPENSES

FOR YEARS ENDED DECEMBER 31, 1962 AND 1963

	1963	Per Cent of Net Sales	1962	Per Cent of Net Sales	Increase-Decrease Amount	Per Cent*
Sales (net)	$563,254		$702,681		$139,427*	19.8*
Salesmen's salaries	$ 57,875	10.3	$ 56,297	8.0	$ 1,578	2.8
Advertising	21,223	3.8	28,515	4.1	7,292*	25.6*
Delivery expense	13,872	2.5	14,685	2.1	813*	5.5*
Salesroom rent	8,400	1.5	7,200	1.0	1,200	16.7
Depreciation of salesroom furniture	3,150	.6	2,056	.3	1,094	53.2
Payroll taxes—selling	2,776	.5	2,582	.4	194	7.5
	$107,296	19.2	$111,335	15.9	$ 4,039*	3.6*

COMMON-SIZE BALANCE SHEET

Some writers have applied the common-size principle to the balance sheet, designating total assets as 100 per cent. The result, however, is not useful. This becomes evident when the notion is applied to the balance sheet of Arthur Milford. On December 31, 1962 the merchandise inventory was 40.7 per cent of total assets and on December 31, 1963 it was 37.6 per cent. Since the inventory increased 3.4 per cent, the common-size percentages obviously do not measure the trend of an item. When read horizontally they measure the trend of the relationship of an item to total assets. But since the total of the assets is affected by the behavior of all the assets, the percentages of the relation of an asset to total assets across the years is too complex for interpretation. In the case under consideration the merchandise inventory percentage decreased because total assets increased, mainly because of the increase in furniture and fixtures, at a higher rate than the merchandise inventory. The use of the common-size balance sheet is therefore not recommended unless in a particular case it can be shown that a norm can be set for the relation of a certain asset to total assets. This, however, is hardly feasible.

MEASUREMENT OF TRENDS

The most satisfactory method for measuring the changes in an item for more than two periods is to state its position in each period as a percentage of its position in the first period taken as the base. In order to do this, the amount of the item in each of the periods is divided by its amount in the first period.

The following are the selling expenses of a certain business:

1959	$110,000
1960	125,000
1961	115,000
1962	90,000
1963	115,000

Applying the method mentioned above, there are obtained the following percentages:

1959	100%
1960	114
1961	105
1962	82
1963	105

These percentages are the ratios of the selling expenses in the various years to the selling expenses in the first year, 1959. Since such ratios measure trends, they are *trend ratios*. They are, in fact, index numbers of the trend.

The question to be answered is whether the trend is satisfactory. The trend by itself does not provide this information. It is necessary to compare it with some other trend to which it bears a logical relationship. Obviously, the selling expenses bear a relationship to sales. Accordingly, the trend of the selling expenses should be compared with that of sales.

The following are the sales figures in the case under consideration:

1959	$750,000
1960	680,000
1961	620,000
1962	645,000
1963	821,000

The trend ratios for these sales figures are:

1959	100%
1960	91
1961	83
1962	86
1963	109

In comparing the trend of the selling expenses with that of the sales, the executive will probably wonder why in 1960 the selling expenses rose to 114 per cent when the sales declined to 91 per cent and why in 1961 the selling expenses declined to only 105 per cent when sales declined to 83 per cent. He can obtain supporting statistics from the accountant and then seek the underlying facts from whoever is in charge of sales operations. Looking further, the executive will see that the selling expenses correlated reasonably with sales in 1962 and 1963.

The trends of all related items in the financial statements may be compared in similar manner.

GRAPHIC REPRESENTATION OF TRENDS

The function of the trend ratios is to simplify the relationships among the figures in the financial statements which are usually too difficult for the mind to comprehend. By plotting the trend ratios on graph paper and thus reducing them to mere lines, the ultimate in simplification is obtained. To illustrate this, the trend ratios of the sales and selling expenses of the case under consideration are plotted in the chart below.

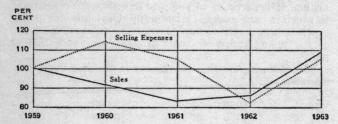

Plotting the trends in dollars would produce the same curves; but if the items compared were in greatly different magnitudes the curves would be far apart. The advantage in plotting the percentages is that the curves will always start at the same point, 100 per cent, and thus enable the eye to compare them more readily. Such graphs are particularly useful when studies are made for many years.*

* For a more elaborate discussion of graphic representation of trends see John N. Myer, *Financial Statement Analysis,* pages 156–171. Englewood Cliffs, N. J.: Prentice-Hall, Inc., 3d edition, 1961.

11. Measurement of Proportions

STRUCTURAL RATIOS

THE FINANCIAL structure of a business is outlined by the fundamental equation of accounting: assets = liabilities + capital. The balance sheet follows the form of this equation and so can be said to set forth the financial structure of a business at a particular date. An important technique of financial statement analysis is that of measuring the proportions within the structure for the purpose of testing whether they are reasonable. The proportions tested are not only those of balance-sheet items to other balance-sheet items but also certain balance-sheet items to income-statement items. These measurements are performed by means of *structural ratios*. An illustration of this has already been given in Chapter 8 where the proportion of current assets to current liabilities was discussed.

RATIO OF CAPITAL TO LIABILITIES

What may be regarded as the most fundamental relationship in the financial structure is the ratio of the capital to the liabilities. This ratio, which is designed to test the proportion of the equity of the owners to that of the creditors, is obtained by dividing the capital by the liabilities. If the result is, say, 3.72, this would indicate a ratio of 3 72/100 to 1, or that the owners had contributed $3.72 of assets for each $1.00 contributed by the creditors.

It should be borne in mind that this measurement, as well as all financial statement measurements, cannot produce precise information since the dollar amounts on which they are based are, as has been explained, the result of conventional procedures implemented by a series of postulates applied with the use of judgment. In some instances the comparison of two items might be affected materially by the price level at the time certain transactions of which the items are the result took place. This would be so in the case of the ratio of capital to liabilities if the greater part of the capital were stated in terms of, say, 1940 dollars and the liabilities in terms of 1964 dollars. But in spite of its lack of precision the comparison is helpful by providing an approximation of the proportions.

It is most convenient to state ratios in the form of percentages. In the case under consideration the ratio of capital to liabilities would be one of 372 per cent. Thus both the structural ratios and the trend ratios are stated in the same manner.

Carrying out the computation of ratios to fractions of a per cent is not useful since the data on which the ratios are based do not have sufficient precision to warrant such procedure. Tenths of a per cent, however, are used in the common-size income statement because the percentages tend to become rather small at the end and rounding off to whole numbers might cause too great a difference.

The computation of ratios is a mechanical process but their interpretation requires considerable understanding and care. The analyst faces the problem of deciding whether a certain ratio is satisfactory or not. But since, because of the lack of precise information given by the dollar amounts it is not possible to set a definite norm, the interpretation must be made by a process of reasoning.

The present discussion of proportions will be limited to commercial and industrial enterprises, thus excluding such types as railroads, public utilities, banks, insurance companies, and so forth, to which the principles here discussed apply but with considerable differences in what proportions are satisfactory. The analysis of the statements of these enterprises had better be discussed in specialized treatises.

Let us now see how the ratio of capital to liabilities can be interpreted. In a commercial or industrial enterprise it is usually to be expected that the capital will be greater than the liabilities. The greater the proportion of the proprietary equity, the more readily can it absorb losses and thus the safer will be the position of the creditors. A ratio of 100 per cent would indicate that the capital and the liabilities were equal. Therefore, for satisfactory proportions the ratio should be above 100 per cent. Accordingly, 100 per cent may be regarded as a *tentative minimum* for this ratio. If it should approach or go below 100 per cent, this would act as a signal which would attract attention to a possible unsatisfactory condition. The analyst, however, should not hasten to come to a conclusion. Rather, he should consider the matter one to be investigated.

Upon investigation it might be found, for example, that the business had been financing its activities to an unusual extent by borrowing and that many of the liabilities are past due. The analyst would consider this an unsatisfactory state of affairs. However, it might be found that although the liabilities are greater than the capital the situation is alleviated by the fact that the biggest creditor is also the biggest stockholder who naturally would not press for payment of the liability to him and thus jeopardize his proprietary interest. In fact, for analytical purposes the liability to this stockholder might well be considered part of the capital.

The foregoing illustrates the fact that a ratio does not give conclusive information. If a ratio is unusual, this does not necessarily indicate that the relationship it measures is unsatisfactory; it merely calls attention to the fact that the relationship requires investigation.

Although the ratio of capital to liabilities should usually be well above 100 per cent, it is not possible to fix a precise percentage and the analyst will have to use his judgment in arriving at a conclusion. And so it is with all the ratios. They do not provide conclusive information. However, the structural ratios are useful in the discovery of disproportions in the financial structure and the trend ratios enable the analyst to observe unusual trends. Having found an unusual ratio, the analyst will proceed to seek the reason for it. Usually this is not to be found in the statements but is available in the accounting records or can be obtained in other ways.

RATIO OF CAPITAL TO NONCURRENT ASSETS

It is reasonable to hold that in a commercial or industrial enterprise the owners should contribute the fundamental framework of the business: the property, plant, and equipment, or fixed assets, and other noncurrent assets. A ratio of 100 per cent would indicate the equality of the capital and noncurrent assets and so constitutes a tentative minimum for this ratio. It should, however, be higher for safe proportions because a ratio of 100 per cent would indicate that the creditors had supplied all of the current assets, which, as will be shown, is not satisfactory.

CURRENT RATIO

The ratio of current assets to current liabilities, commonly known as the current ratio, is used as the first step in the analysis of current position or debt-paying ability. It compares the current debts, that is, debts payable in not more than one year, with what the business has or will have available to pay these debts. Of course, liabilities are paid in cash. But usually all the liabilities are not due immediately. In the course of time merchandise will be sold and receivables collected, thus providing cash. The current ratio, therefore, constitutes an overall measure of debt-paying ability.

For reasonable proportions the current assets should be expected to be greater than the current liabilities because losses commonly occur in both receivables and merchandise while liabilities are not likely to decrease. But how much greater should the current assets be than the current liabilities?

At the turn of the century the bankers developed the notion that for safe proportions the current assets should be at least twice the current liabilities. The 2 to 1 or 200 per cent ratio became widely accepted and is commonly referred to in financial literature. This, however, is a rather arbitrary rule. Although in many cases if the current assets are twice the current liabilities the current position is satisfactory, there are many instances in which the 2 to 1 ratio does not afford a reliable norm.

What constitutes a satisfactory current ratio depends on the relative rate of collection of revenue and payment of liabilities. A business conducted on the cash basis collects revenue as soon as a sale is made and so its current assets do not contain receivables. From this it follows that its current ratio may normally be lower than the current ratio of a business that extends credit and carries receivables among its current assets. The same applies to a business that sells on credit but collects its revenue before it has to pay for the goods sold, as, for example, if it sells on 30-day terms and buys on 90-day terms. On the other hand, a business that is required to pay for merchandise or materials before it can collect its revenue will require a higher current ratio.

It is thus evident that a norm such as that of 200 per cent is not generally applicable. However, since in many cases if the current assets are twice the current liabilities, it is likely that the proportions are satisfactory, this ratio may be used as a starting point for consideration of current position. Then, if the ratio is above 200 per cent it may be regarded as on the stronger side and when below 200 per cent on the weaker side. This is rather inconclusive but it is only the first step in the analysis of current position; several other steps are necessary.

WORKING CAPITAL AND CURRENT RATIO

Two measures of liquidity have been mentioned: (1) working capital, the excess of current assets over current liabilities, and (2) the ratio of the current assets to the current liabilities. A comparison of the two is afforded by the following illustration.

The balance sheets of Company X and Company Y show:

	Company X	Company Y
Current assets	$180,000	$30,000
Current liabilities	120,000	15,000
Working capital	$ 60,000	$15,000

Upon computing the current ratios of these companies, it is found that Company X's is 150 per cent and Company Y's is 200 per cent. This signifies that for each dollar of current liabilities, Company X has $1.50 of current assets, while Company Y has $2.00 of current assets. From this it is evident that the current ratio is the better measure of debt-paying ability. Obviously, the greater working capital of Company X is due to the fact that this company's current assets and current liabilities are on a larger scale than those of Company Y. The measure of working capital thus gives an indication of size, a fact obscured in the current ratio.

Both measures may be used since they provide different information.

It follows that an increase in working capital does not necessarily indicate increased debt-paying ability. This is demonstrated by comparing the working capital of Company Y with its working capital the following year in which it increased to $30,000, the current assets amounting to $90,000 and the current liabilities to $60,000. But the current ratio declined to 150 per cent.

ACID TEST

It is sometimes found in a merchandising business that the current ratio is very high but the situation poor because the current assets contain too great an amount of inventory, a condition called *overinventoried*. In order to check on this possibility, a supplement to the current ratio is used. It is in the form of the ratio of "quick" current assets to current liabilities. The "quick" current assets usually consist of cash and receivables but might in a large business include investments in marketable securities, sometimes referred to as "near-cash."

In the course of time 100 per cent became the accepted minimum for this ratio. It was, however, conceded that this was a rather stringent rule, so that the ratio became known as *the acid test*. The analyst will interpret the acid test ratio in the light of the facts available.

RECEIVABLES AND SALES

An important consideration is whether the receivables are collected in accordance with the terms of sale. This may be done by comparing the sales for the year with the receivables shown in the balance sheet at the end of the year. For this the ratio of sales to receivables may be used.

To illustrate: if the sales for a year amount to $439,467 and the receivables on December 31 of that year are $73,692, the ratio of sales to receivables is one of about 600 per cent, indicating that the sales were six times the receivables on December 31 or that one-sixth of the sales for the year had not been collected. If there were about 300 business days during the year, fifty days' sales had not been collected. If the terms of sale are 30 days net, then collections are approximately 20 days behind.

A convenient substitute for the ratio of sales to receivables is the number of days' sales contained in the receivables. Applying it to the foregoing case, the year's sales, $439,467, is divided by 300, making the average sales per day $1,465. Dividing the receivables, $73,692, by $1,465, there is obtained about 50 days' sales contained in the receivables.

It should be observed that there is an assumption in this calculation that the sales are made at a reasonably constant rate throughout the year. In many cases this is not so. In a business with considerable seasonality the calculation has no validity. At best, it is a rough approximation and has significance only when it indicates a considerable discrepancy such as, in the present case, 20 days.

INVENTORY AND SALES

It is important to know whether the inventory of merchandise, in a merchandising business, or of finished goods, in a manufacturing business, is in reasonable proportion to the sales volume. Since the inventory is stated more or less with relation to cost and the sales are on a cost plus profit basis, comparison would not yield useful results. A better comparison for the purpose is that of the sales on the cost basis, that is, the cost of goods sold, for the year, with the average inventory carried during the year.

To illustrate: if the cost of goods sold during a year amounted to $740,395 and the average inventory was $92,567, then, dividing $740,395 by $92,567, it is found that the average inventory was sold out about 8 times during the year, or every 1½ months, an *inventory turnover* of 8 times.

The analyst will consider this rate in the light of what he believes normal for the type of business. There are many differences in the rates of turnover. To take two extremes: a news-stand will turn over its stock 365 times a year, while a jeweler might be glad if his stock turns over once a year.

The difficulty in computing the rate of turnover lies in obtaining the average inventory. If a perpetual inventory system is used it is possible to have monthly figures and so a representative average may be obtained by totaling the 12 inventories and dividing by 12. But where the periodic inventory method is used, which is usually the case in a small business, only an annual inventory figure is available and the average will be obtained by adding the initial and the final inventories and dividing the total by 2. This may not be representative for the year, particularly if the type of business is seasonal. So that, again, the analyst must interpret the results of the calculation in the light of the facts available about the business.

RETURN ON CAPITAL

The rate of return on the investment in a business measures the ultimate goal of operations since business is organized to earn income. The ratio of net income for the year to the capital invested provides the desired measure. In this calculation the capital at the beginning or end of the year or the average capital during the year, if available, may be used, at the discretion of the analyst. Thus, if the capital is $105,297 and the net income for the year $15,825, the rate of return is one of about 15 per cent.

A variant of this calculation, in order to check the rate of return on the investment in property, plant, and equipment in an industrial enterprise, is to divide the net income by the investment in property, plant, and equipment. This measure may be used to appraise the management's efficiency in the use of capital invested in the facilities used in operations.

Here, again, the price-level problem enters. The net income is stated in current dollars while the investment, particularly in property, plant, and equipment, may have been made in dollars having quite a different purchasing power. Care must be exercised in interpreting the percentage of return on capital.*

* Those interested in the matter of price-level adjustment of financial statements are referred to John N. Myer, *Financial Statement Analysis*, Chapter 4. Englewood Cliffs, N. J.: Prentice-Hall, Inc., 3d edition, 1961.

    An interesting study of the subject is that of Ralph Coughenour Jones, *Effects of Price Level Changes on Business Income, Capital and Taxes*, American Accounting Association, 1956.

NET WORTH

Analysts who are not familiar with the principles of accounting are inclined to use the term *net worth* to designate the proprietary equity or capital of a business. This expression is avoided by accountants because of its misleading connotation that the sum so designated indicates what the business is worth, that is, what might be realized if the business were sold. The reader will by now understand that this is by no means so.

The term could reasonably be used, for example, in the case of one John Smith whose only asset is $6,000 cash and who has liabilities amounting to $2,000. His "net worth" might then be said to be $4,000. But to apply the term to a case in which there are many kinds of assets and liabilities is unsatisfactory.

CHECKING THE DANGER SPOTS

It will have been observed from the foregoing that the function of the structural ratios is to check the "danger spots," those points at which disproportions commonly occur. These are:

> The equities
> Noncurrent assets
> Receivables
> Inventory
> Net income

In using the structural ratios the analyst performs a series of tests. If he considers a ratio satisfactory he regards the result a negative one and passes on to the next test. When he encounters an unsatisfactory ratio the result of the test is positive and the matter is placed on a list of items to be investigated. The manner of the investigation will depend on whether the analyst is inside or outside the business. If on the inside he will have access to the accounting and other records; if on the outside he may or may not be able to obtain the facts. But if, for example, the analyst should be a bank credit man and the business desires a loan the management will no doubt be willing to answer questions. The case studies in the following chapter will illustrate the use of ratios as a means to the discovery of facts about a business.

ILLOGICAL RATIOS

The structural ratios that have been discussed measure relationships which are obviously meaningful. The analyst will in certain kinds of business find others that have significance but which do not apply to all types. There is no limit to the comparisons that may be made among the financial statement items as long as there is a significant relationship between the items compared.

The literature of financial statement analysis abounds with suggested ratios which have no logical basis. The ratio of current assets to fixed assets, for example, can serve no purpose since it is impossible to determine what the proportion of the stated dollars of current assets should be to the stated dollars of fixed assets. Also, who can say what should be the proportion of working capital on the last day of the year to the sales or the net income for the year?

TRENDS OF STRUCTURAL RATIOS

The study of the trends of various structural ratios has been suggested. The trend of a structural ratio is the trend of the relationship of two entities. The information it provides is rather superficial since it does not throw light on the relative behavior of the two entities. This is readily seen in the case of the trend of the current ratio. It is not sufficient, for example, to know that the ratio rose; it is more important to know why it rose. The rise may have been caused by:

1. A rise in current assets and a decline in current liabilities.

2. A rise in both current assets and current liabilities, but the rise in current assets at a higher rate than that in current liabilities.

3. A decline in both current assets and current liabilities,

but the decline in current liabilities at a higher rate than that in current assets.

The observation of the trends of the two variables will disclose their relative behavior which resulted in the relationship at the last date or for the last period.

STANDARD RATIOS

The most difficult problem in the use of structural ratios is to establish norms which will make it possible to know when the ratios are satisfactory and when they are not. This need has been felt since the beginning of the use of ratio analysis of financial statements more than half a century ago. In order to satisfy this want, various writers have advanced the idea that a standard could be obtained by collecting a representative group of statements for each type business, computing a series of ratios therefrom, and taking an average of each of the ratios. These average or standard ratios, they have held, would be guides to a decision regarding whether a certain enterprise is at, above, or below the average for the kind of business in which it is engaged. The idea, however, is not feasible.

In the first place, it is difficult to make a simple classification of types of business. This is easily seen from a perusal of the *Census of Manufactures* of the U. S. Bureau of the Census. One might speak of the "textile industry." But the Bureau lists 32 types under this head. Granted that one has compiled a list of companies in one of the groups, he faces the question whether all members of the group use the same accounting procedure. With respect to the inventory, for example, do they all use FIFO, LIFO, the average cost method, or some other method? Then there is the price-level problem in the matter of the acquisition of fixed assets. Did these companies acquire their property, plant, and equipment on the same price level so that these assets are stated in the same kind of dollars? Differences in the price level at date of acquisition would, of course, affect the depreciation figure also. Do they all follow the same managerial policies? For instance, do they all own the buildings occupied or do they rent them? There are so many differences among enterprises, even in the same industrial classification, that averages obtained from their financial statements are averages of unlike things and therefore have no validity.

As will be demonstrated in the next chapter, a self-contained method of deciding on the satisfactoriness of a structural ratio is the only feasible one.

12. Case Studies

IN ORDER TO illustrate the application of the analytical methods outlined in the previous chapter, three-year comparative statements of four enterprises will be analyzed in this chapter. In each case it is assumed that the analysis is performed as of the latest balance-sheet date. Therefore, only the structural ratios at this date are used, together with the trend ratios that show the movement of the various items to arrive at the relationships measured by the structural ratios. These vertical and horizontal measures are complementary and constitute an integrated system of analysis. Included in the analysis is a comparative common-size income statement which provides both a vertical and horizontal analysis of the distribution of the average sales dollar, one of the most useful kinds of information.

As has been explained, the ratios are not conclusive. Their function is to call attention to what is unusual. Unusual trends and proportions may be either favorable or unfavorable. Their evaluation can be effected only as the result of a fact-finding process. Since every transaction of a financial nature is reflected in the financial statement items, the analyst must attempt to get the facts behind the figures. Getting the facts will depend on whether he has access to the accounting records or to what extent the management is willing to give him information. If he cannot obtain facts, the only result of his analysis will be a knowledge of what is unusual in the case. Of course, sometimes the facts may be surmised.

Each analysis is followed by an interpretation concluding with a summary of the information to be sought and suggestions as to what the facts might be.

The reader should not become discouraged by the volume of calculations in these illustrations. For the purpose of expounding the principles involved, the analyses have been made the long, hard way. With a little practice, the analyst will develop the ability to spot unusual trends and proportions without actually calculating any ratios, particularly in the case of a small business.

CASE NO. 1

G. T. ARTHUR

COMPARATIVE BALANCE SHEET
DECEMBER 31

Assets	1963	1962	1961
Cash	$ 44,297	$ 13,185	$ 23,723
Accounts receivable (less bad debts estimate)	27,348	49,183	44,198
Merchandise inventory	98,150	73,598	67,849
Prepaid expenses	3,505	1,845	1,056
Total current assets	$173,300	$137,811	$136,826
Furniture and equipment (less depreciation)	110,740	98,655	92,720
	$284,040	$236,466	$229,546

Liabilities and Capital			
Notes payable (bank)	$ 10,000	$ 7,000	$ 2,000
Accounts payable	83,745	52,380	51,725
Accrued expenses	4,750	3,087	1,562
Total current liabilities	$ 98,495	$ 62,467	$ 55,287
G. T. Arthur, Capital	185,545	173,999	174,259
	$284,040	$236,466	$229,546

COMPARATIVE INCOME STATEMENT
FOR YEAR'S ENDED DECEMBER 31

	1963	1962	1961
Sales (net)	$437,570	$372,860	$348,173
Cost of goods sold	258,645	224,532	210,328
Gross margin	$178,925	$148,328	$137,845
Expenses (less other income)	162,587	134,983	120,164
Net income for the year	$ 16,338	$ 13,345	$ 17,681

G. T. Arthur is a wholesaler of paper products. His terms of sale are 1/10, net 30 days.

ANALYSIS

Trend Ratios

December 31 or Year Ended December 31

	1961	1962	1963
Current assets	100%	101%	127%
Current liabilities	100	113	178
Receivables	100	111	62
Merchandise inventory	100	108	145
Sales	100	107	126
Cost of goods sold	100	107	123
Expenses	100	112	135
Net income	100	75	92
Capital	100	100	106
Noncurrent assets	100	106	119

Structural Ratios, December 31, 1963

Current ratio	176%
Acid test	73
Capital to liabilities	188
Capital to noncurrent assets	168
Net income to capital	9
Days' sales in receivables	App. 19 days
Inventory turnover	App. 3 times

Comparative Common-Size Income Statement
For Years Ended December 31

	1963	1962	1961
Sales (net)	100.0%	100.0%	100.0%
Cost of goods sold	59.1	60.2	60.4
Gross margin	40.9%	39.8%	39.6%
Expenses (less other income)	37.2	36.2	34.5
Net income for the year	3.7%	3.6%	5.1%

INTERPRETATION

The current position of this business has become constantly less favorable since December 31, 1961, as indicated by the trends of the current assets and current liabilities, the current liabilities rising to 178 per cent of their position at December 31, 1961 while the current assets rose to only 127 per cent. The current ratio of 176 per cent is weak, as is also the acid test of 73 per cent. The low acid test ratio leads one to expect a relatively large inventory.

The trend of the inventory to 145 per cent of its position at December 31, 1961 confirms the expectation of heaviness. This upward trend is in sharp contrast to the trend of sales to only 126 per cent. The turnover of 3 times is low for the type of business.

Improvement in the rate of collection of receivables is indicated by the trend of receivables, although the days' sales in receivables of approximately 19 is somewhat high in the light of the 10-day discount offered.

Although sales rose to 126 per cent of their 1961 volume, this rise was accompanied by a lesser rise in cost of goods sold to 123 per cent. The comparative common-size income statement shows that in 1961, 60.4 cents of the average sales dollar was used to pay for the goods sold. This declined to 60.2 cents in 1962 and to 59.1 cents in 1963. This is favorable.

However, the constant rise in the expenses from 34.5 cents of the average sales dollar in 1961, to 36.2 cents in 1962, and 37.2 cents in 1963 is unfavorable. The effect of the increase in the expense of operating the business offset the increase in gross margin which was the result of the decrease in cost of goods sold per dollar of sales, thus causing a decline in the net income per average sales dollar from 5.1 cents in 1961 to 3.6 cents in 1962, with a slight rise to 3.7 cents in 1963.

In 1962 the trend of the net income declined to 75 per cent of that in 1961 and in 1963 rose to 92 per cent. The net income on the capital as of December 31, 1963 was 9 per cent. However, since the business is an individual proprietorship the capital is subject to constant change. Information regarding the average capital during the year is not available.

The comparative balance sheet shows a constant increase in furniture and equipment, probably on account of improvements—a progressive indication.

The ratios of capital to liabilities and capital to noncurrent assets are quite satisfactory.

CONCLUSION

The analysis reveals three matters requiring investigation:

1. Heavy current liabilities.
2. Large inventory.
3. Increase in operating expenses.

The heavy current liabilities are undoubtedly due to the purchase of inventory or fixed assets or both. The business has a considerable amount of cash available to take care of immediate payments.

The critical question is how soon the inventory will be sold. Investigation might reveal that Mr. Arthur anticipated the receipt of large orders but that this did not materialize. Therefore, he faces the serious problem of disposing of his stock. It might, however, be found that there is a definite indication that sales will increase materially in January. In such case the inventory position might be quite satisfactory.

Explanation should be sought for the increase in the operating expenses. It should be ascertained which of the expenses increased and the reason therefor. The increase may or may not be justified.

CASE NO. 2

GEORGE HICKMAN
COMPARATIVE BALANCE SHEET
DECEMBER 31

Assets	1963	1962	1961
Cash	$ 20,842	$ 15,326	$ 10,173
Accounts receivable (less bad debts estimate)	92,520	65,673	42,875
Merchandise inventory	65,737	67,342	72,586
Prepaid expenses	2,843	1,528	920
Total current assets	$181,942	$149,869	$126,554
Fixed assets (less depreciation)	$105,848	$104,347	$102,590
Sundry investments	8,000	7,500	5,000
Total noncurrent assets	$113,848	$111,847	$107,590
	$295,790	$261,716	$234,144

Liabilities and Capital			
Accounts payable	$ 70,356	$ 66,342	$ 58,705
Accrued expenses	2,820	2,047	1,245
Total current liabilities	$ 73,176	$ 68,389	$ 59,950
George Hickman, Capital	222,614	193,327	174,194
	$295,790	$261,716	$234,144

COMPARATIVE INCOME STATEMENT
FOR YEARS ENDED DECEMBER 31

	1963	1962	1961
Sales (net)	$512,850	$487,390	$425,683
Cost of goods sold	331,258	293,725	245,072
Gross margin	$181,592	$193,665	$180,611
Expenses (less other income)	150,722	147,105	128,564
Net income for the year	$ 30,870	$ 46,560	$ 52,047

George Hickman is a distributor of electrical supplies. His terms of sale are 30 days net.

ANALYSIS

Trend Ratios
December 31 or Year Ended December 31

	1961	1962	1963
Current assets	100%	118%	144%
Current liabilities	100	114	122
Receivables	100	153	216
Merchandise inventory	100	93	91
Sales	100	114	120
Cost of goods sold	100	120	135
Expenses	100	114	117
Net income	100	89	59
Capital	100	111	128
Noncurrent assets	100	104	106

Structural Ratios, December 31, 1963

Current ratio	249%
Acid test	155
Capital to liabilities	304
Capital to noncurrent assets	196
Net income to capital	14
Days' sales in receivables	App. 54 days
Inventory turnover	App. 5 times

Comparative Common-Size Income Statement
For Years Ended December 31

	1963	1962	1961
Sales (net)	100.0%	100.0%	100.0%
Cost of goods sold	64.6	60.3	57.6
Gross margin	35.4%	39.7%	42.4%
Expenses (less other income)	29.4	30.2	30.2
Net income for the year	6.0%	9.5%	12.2%

INTERPRETATION

Because of the greater increase in current assets than in current liabilities, the current position of this business has constantly become stronger since December 31, 1961. The current ratio of 249 per cent and the acid test ratio of 155 per cent as of December 31, 1963 are satisfactory according to tentative standards.

The constant greater rise in receivables than in sales since December 31, 1961 causes concern. The days' sales in receivables of 54 at December 31, 1963 indicates heaviness in the light of the terms of 30 days net.

The trend of the inventory in relation to sales appears satisfactory since sales have constantly increased while inventory has constantly decreased. The turnover of 5 times seems reasonable.

Cost of goods sold rose to 135 per cent of 1961 level, while sales rose to only 120 per cent. Turning to the comparative common-size income statement, one sees that in 1961 the cost per dollar of sales was 57.6 cents, in 1962, 60.3 cents, and in 1963, 64.6 cents. This is unfavorable.

On the other hand, the trend of the operating expenses, although upward, moved at a much lower rate than that of sales: to 117 per cent. In contrast, the common-size figures show 30.2 cents per dollar of sales in both 1961 and 1962 and a slight decline to 29.4 cents in 1963. The rise in cost of goods sold was thus partly offset by a decline in expenses in 1963.

However, net income per dollar of sales declined from 12.2 cents in 1961 to 9.5 cents in 1962 and 6.0 cents in 1963. Although the trend of the net income declined to 59 per cent of its 1961 level, the rate of return on the stated capital as of December 31, 1963 was 14 per cent, a still reasonable figure. But, of course, since this business is in the form of an individual proprietorship, the capital may have varied considerably during the year.

The ratios of capital to liabilities of 304 per cent and capital to noncurrent assets of 196 per cent are satisfactory.

CONCLUSION

The analysis has revealed two matters requiring investigation:

1. Heavy receivables.
2. Constant rise in the cost of goods sold.

The usual procedure for an analysis of receivables is in the form of an "aging." This consists chiefly of a review of the amounts not yet due and the amounts past due. The investigation might show that Mr. Hickman has had difficulty in making collections and that many accounts are past due. This would be unfavorable. However, it might be found that there are no accounts past due and that the large amount of receivables is the result of the fact that during the last month of the year sales were unusually high. This would be most favorable.

The rise in the cost of goods sold should be accounted for. It should be ascertained whether the rise was caused by inefficient purchasing or by an increase in the price level. If due to inefficient purchasing, correction of the inefficiency is indicated. If caused by a rise in the price level, it should be determined whether selling prices might be increased in line with cost prices. It should be noted in this connection that in a period of rising prices it is a common phenomenon that costs rise before selling prices can be adjusted.

The nature of the "sundry investments" should be determined.

CASE NO. 3

MULTIPLAST CORPORATION
COMPARATIVE BALANCE SHEET
DECEMBER 31

Assets	1963	1962	1961
Cash	$ 48,729	$ 17,652	$ 6,845
Accounts receivable (less allowance for bad debts)	105,826	102,103	103,782
Raw materials (at the lower of LIFO cost or market)	65,640	52,781	48,359
Work in process (at cost)	23,529	24,658	20,752
Finished goods (at LIFO cost)	130,975	87,365	85,942
Prepaid expenses	8,526	6,745	6,240
Total current assets	$383,225	$291,304	$271,920
Property, plant, and equipment (less depreciation)	$112,685	$ 87,001	$ 79,362
Miscellaneous receivables (not current)	4,870	3,450	—
Total noncurrent assets	$117,555	$ 90,451	$ 79,362
	$500,780	$381,755	$351,282

Liabilities, Capital Stock, and Retained Earnings

Notes payable (bank)	$ 15,000	$ 5,000	$ —
Accounts payable	162,716	72,592	$56,010
Dividends payable	10,000	10,000	10,000
Federal income taxes payable	27,699	43,457	45,725
Accrued expenses	10,570	7,057	6,590
Total current liabilities	$225,985	$138,106	$118,325
Loan payable (due January 1, 1965)	35,000	—	—
Total liabilities	$260,985	$138,106	$118,325
Capital stock—common, par $100	$200,000	$200,000	$200,000
Retained earnings	39,795	43,649	32,957
Total capital	$239,795	$243,649	$232,957
	$500,780	$381,755	$351,282

COMPARATIVE INCOME STATEMENT
FOR YEARS ENDED DECEMBER 31

	1963	1962	1961
Sales (net)	$920,362	$785,904	$702,613
Cost of goods sold	440,763	377,235	335,920
Gross margin	$479,599	$408,669	$366,693
Expenses (less other income)	415,754	314,520	268,182
Net income before federal income taxes	$ 63,845	$ 94,149	$ 98,511
Federal income taxes	27,699	43,457	45,725
Net income for the year	$ 36,146	$ 50,692	$ 52,786
Dividends	$ 40,000	$ 40,000	$ 40,000

The Multiplast Corporation is a manufacturer of plastics. Its terms of sale are 30 days net.

ANALYSIS

Trend Ratios
December 31 or Year Ended December 31

	1961	1962	1963
Current assets	100%	107%	141%
Current liabilities	100	117	191
Receivables	100	98	102
Inventory of finished goods	100	102	152
Sales	100	112	131
Cost of goods sold	100	112	131
Expenses (less other income)	100	117	155
Net income	100	96	68
Capital	100	105	103
Noncurrent assets	100	114	148
Total liabilities	100	117	221

Structural Ratios, December 31, 1963

Current ratio	170%
Acid test	68
Capital to liabilities	92
Capital to noncurrent assets	204
Net income to capital	15
Days' sales in receivables	App. 35 days
Inventory turnover (finished goods)	App. 4 times

Comparative Common-Size Income Statement
For Years Ended December 31

	1963	1962	1961
Sales (net)	100.0%	100.0%	100.0%
Cost of goods sold	47.9	48.0	47.8
Gross margin	52.1%	52.0%	52.2%
Expenses (less other income)	45.2	40.0	38.2
Net income before federal income taxes	6.9%	12.0%	14.0%
Federal income taxes	3.0	5.5	6.5
Net income for the year	3.9%	6.5%	7.5%

INTERPRETATION

The current position of this company has constantly become less favorable since December 31, 1961 because of the stronger upward trend in current liabilities than in current assets, particularly at December 31, 1963. Both the current ratio of 170 per cent and the acid test ratio of 68 per cent indicate poor current position. The latter ratio points to a high inventory.

There is little variation in the trend of the receivables and the days' sales in receivables, allowing for lack of precision of the measure, seems satisfactory.

The rise in the trend of the inventory of finished goods as of December 31, 1963 to 152 per cent, while sales rose to only 131 per cent during 1963, attracts attention. The turnover of 4 times is rather low.

The trend of the cost of goods sold is identical with that of the sales. However, the trend of the operating expenses has been rising at a higher rate than that of sales, to 155 per cent, while sales rose to 131 per cent. Common-size figures show that the expenses were 38.2 cents of the average sales dollar in 1961, 40.0 cents in 1962, and 45.2 cents in 1963.

The rise in expenses was the chief cause of the decline in net income to 96 per cent in 1962 and 68 per cent in 1963. This decline is also seen in the common-size figures which show that the net income per dollar of sales declined from 7.5 cents in 1961 to 6.5 cents in 1962 and to 3.9 cents in 1963. However, the rate of return of 15 per cent on the capital in 1963 is rather good. The corporation has been able to pay the same rate of dividends for the three years.

The increase in noncurrent assets (mainly property, plant, and equipment) is probably due to modernization. The ratio of capital to noncurrent assets is satisfactory.

The trend of total liabilities in 1963 to 221 per cent of their position at December 31, 1961 attracts attention. The greater rise in total liabilities than in current liabilities was caused by a long-term loan amounting to $35,000.

The ratio of capital to liabilities of 92 per cent indicates that the equity of the creditors is greater than that of the owners.

CONCLUSION

The analysis has revealed the following to be investigated:

1. Heavy liabilities.
2. Insufficient capital.
3. The nature of the long-term loan.
4. Large inventory of finished goods.
5. Increase in operating expenses.

The current position of this company is very poor. The current ratio is low by any reasonable standards, there being only $1.70 of current assets to each $1.00 of current liabilities and 57 per cent of the current assets consists of inventory. The current liabilities are undoubtedly to a large extent for purchase of inventory and possibly also for improvement of facilities.

The ratio of capital to liabilities of 92 per cent registers a danger signal. The total of the liabilities includes a $35,000 long-term loan due in 2 years. Investigation with respect to the source of the loan might reveal that it was obtained from a stockholder. In such case, for analytical purposes the loan might be considered part of the proprietary equity, so that the ratio of capital to liabilities would be raised to 122 per cent.

The large inventory of finished goods is the outstanding problem. Investigation might disclose that the management expected a large demand for its products and entered into an accelerated production program. Unfortunately, its anticipations were not realized and there are no indications that they will be realized in the near future. The situation is therefore, very bad. However, it might be found that the company has advance orders for delivery in the near future and that production was increased to fill these orders. The situation would thus be very bright. The conversion of the inventory into cash with which to pay the liabilities would, of course, correct the current position.

There remains the matter of the increase in operating expenses. It should be ascertained which of the expenses increased and what can be done to decrease them in the future. On the other hand, it should be determined whether sales prices can be increased.

Earnings for 1963 were 15 per cent on capital. But it is obvious that the capital is too small for carrying on operations. If the $35,000 loan were considered part of the capital, the return on capital would be one of 13 per cent, which is still reasonable.

CASE NO. 4
RELIABLE FIXIT SHOP
COMPARATIVE BALANCE SHEET
AUGUST 31

Assets	1964	1963	1962
Cash	$ 3,127	$ 2,892	$2,075
Accounts receivable	1,226	1,024	825
Supplies	5,042	4,528	3,720
Prepaid expenses	1,563	1,042	985
Total current assets	$10,958	$ 9,486	$7,605
Furniture and equipment (less depreciation)	3,542	3,729	2,354
	$14,500	$13,215	$9,959

Liabilities and Capital			
Accounts payable	$ 4,026	$ 3,423	$2,956
Accrued expenses	1,250	962	873
Total current liabilities	$ 5,276	$ 4,385	$3,829
J. A. Rivera, Capital	$ 4,612	$ 4,415	$3,065
L. S. Santos, Capital	4,612	4,415	3,065
Total capital	$ 9,224	$ 8,830	$6,130
	$14,500	$13,215	$9,959

COMPARATIVE INCOME STATEMENT
FOR YEARS ENDED AUGUST 31

	1964	1963	1962
Service charges	$99,762	$103,720	$125,263
Cost of services	70,947	70,168	83,132
Gross margin	$28,815	$ 33,552	$ 42,131
Operating expenses	8,467	8,483	8,530
Net income for the year	$20,348	$ 25,069	$ 33,601

The Reliable Fixit Shop is operated by the partnership of Rivera and Santos, specializing in household repairs. Terms: bills due when rendered.

ANALYSIS

Trend Ratios

August 31 or Year Ended August 31

	1962	1963	1964
Current assets	100%	125%	144%
Current liabilities	100	115	138
Receivables		Not significant	
Service charges	100	83	80
Cost of services	100	84	85
Operating expenses	100	99	99
Net income	100	75	61
Capital	100	144	150
Noncurrent assets	100	158	150

Strucural Ratios, August 31, 1964

Current ratio	208%
Acid test	Not applicable
Capital to liabilities	175
Capital to noncurrent assets	260
Net income to capital	221

Comparative Common-Size Income Statement
For Years Ended August 31

	1964	1963	1962
Service charges	100.0%	100.0%	100.0%
Cost of services	71.1	67.7	66.4
Gross margin	28.9%	32.3%	33.6%
Operating expenses	8.5	8.2	6.8
Net income for the year	20.4%	24.1%	26.8%

INTERPRETATION

This partnership has a satisfactory current position. Both current assets and current liabilities have increased since August 31, 1962, the current assets rising at a higher rate than the current liabilities. The current ratio of 208 per cent meets tentative requirements, particularly since this business is more or less on a cash basis. Because the business does not sell goods, the acid test is not applicable.

The ratios of capital to liabilities and capital to noncurrent assets are satisfactory.

The revenue from service charges has declined to 80 per cent of its amount in year ended August 31, 1962. The situation was worsened, as indicated by the common-size figures, by a constant rise in cost of services: 66.4 cents per dollar of revenue, to 67.7 cents, to 71.1 cents; and a constant rise in operating expenses: 6.8 cents, to 8.2 cents, to 8.5 cents.

The rise in deductions from revenue has caused a decline in net income to 61 per cent of its amount for year ended August 31, 1962. Common-size figures show a decline in net income per dollar of service charges from 26.8 cents, to 24.1 cents, to 20.4 cents. The return on stated capital as of August 31, 1964 is 221 per cent. This, however, is not a satisfactory measure in this case since the investment is small. It would appear from the small amount of operating expenses that the partners have no employees and that their contribution to the business is both in the form of capital and labor. The income of about $10,000 a year to each of the partners cannot be regarded as high.

CONCLUSION

An investigation should be made to determine whether service charges, cost of services, and operating expenses cannot be adjusted in order to increase earnings.

13. Manufacturing Costs: Historical

THE SCHEDULE of cost of goods sold illustrated on pages 46–47 shows how in a manufacturing business the cost of the goods manufactured during a year is arrived at. However, for the manufacturing executive this cost information is too little and comes too late. It comes too late because in most cases the accountant cannot supply it until a month or more after the end of the year; it is too little because the executive requires more detailed information, not only at the end but also during the year.

NEED FOR DETAILED COST INFORMATION

Since there is hardly a business that manufactures only one uniform commodity, information regarding the cost of production of each of those manufactured is necessary. Not only this, but the *unit cost* of each commodity is important. For example, a manufacturer of machinery needs to know the cost of production of one machine, the manufacturer of men's shirts the cost of one shirt, and the manufacturer of soap the cost of one cake. Further, the manufacturer would like to have an analysis of the unit cost into the three elements of cost: direct materials, direct labor, and manufacturing overhead. And when the product moves through several stages of production, management wants to know the unit cost of each of the three elements in each stage.

Cost data are used for the purpose of inventory pricing, cost control, and as a basis for decisions regarding selling prices and possible change or discontinuance of a product that cannot in its present form be sold at a profitable margin above cost.

COST ACCOUNTING

In order to provide detailed cost information, accountants have devised a system of record-keeping known as *cost accounting* which constitutes an analytical supplement to what is usually called *general* or *financial accounting*.

Cost accounting systems are adapted to the type of manufacturing in which they are used. In industries such as clothing, furniture, and printing, goods are usually manufactured on specific orders. Therefore, the enterprises in these industries use a type of cost accounting procedure that is called *job order* cost accounting. Under a job order system a record is kept of the cost of the direct materials, the direct labor, and the indirect manufacturing expenses, or manufacturing overhead, allocated to each order, or job lot, or batch of product. The total is the cost of the job which when divided by the number of units produced gives the *unit cost* of production.

In industries such as cement, paint, textiles, and chemicals where there is a continuous mass production of uniform products, a type of cost system is employed known as *process* cost accounting. Under the process cost accounting method the costs are accumulated by process or stages in production instead of by jobs. The total of the costs of a product accumulated in a period of time, usually a month, in each process divided by the number of units produced in that process gives the unit cost of production in the process for the period; and the total of the unit costs of all the processes is the unit cost of the product.

Job order and process cost accounting may be on a *historical cost* basis or on a *standard cost* basis. Historical costs are determined from the record of the *actual* cost of production whereas standard costs are obtained from a predetermined estimate of what the product *should* cost. Historical costs will be discussed in this chapter and predetermined costs in the next chapter.

Job Order Cost Accounting

In a job order system each job is distinguished by a number or other symbol, or combination of both, and a record in the form of a *job cost sheet* is kept on the cost of each job. On this sheet are recorded the (direct) material, (direct) labor, and overhead cost of the job. In order to accumulate this information it is necessary to have systematic procedure in the factory. This procedure will now be summarized.

MATERIAL

A cost accounting system requires that the perpetual inventory method, as explained on pages 39–40, be used in handling materials. When material is required by the factory, a requisition form is filled out giving a description of the material, the department requiring it, and the job on which it is to be used. The requisition is then sent to the storeroom where the storekeeper prices it in accordance with the inventory method in use: FIFO, LIFO, or other. The priced requisition is then employed as the basis for the entry on the appropriate job cost sheet.

LABOR

The labor cost of the various jobs in process is obtained from the payroll records in which the wages paid are analyzed according to the jobs on which the labor was used. This information is carried to the labor section of the appropriate job cost sheets.

OVERHEAD

It is not difficult to keep records of the material and labor used on each job. But it is not so easy to determine how much of the depreciation of the building and machinery, the taxes on the building, and the electricity consumed should be apportioned to each job. Nor can it readily be said how much of the (indirect) labor of foremen, repairmen, and porters, and the cost of the (indirect) material such as fuel, oil, and other supplies belongs to each of the various jobs.

In order to apportion or apply the overhead costs of the factory to the jobs, accountants have developed a conventional procedure which is the one in common use. According to this method the overhead to be applied is calculated on some predetermined basis. The most usual method is to apply the overhead in proportion to the amount of direct labor hours spent on each job. This is quite logical since so many of the indirect costs such as depreciation, taxes, electricity, and fuel accumulate with the passage of time. The assignment of the overhead to a job is performed by using a rate per labor hour predetermined commonly at the beginning of each year on the basis of an estimate or budget. The estimated amount of overhead that will be incurred during the year is divided by the estimated number of direct labor hours to obtain the rate of overhead application. Thus if it is estimated in a certain factory that the overhead for the year will amount to $240,000 and that 80,000 direct labor hours will be required, the rate of overhead application will be $240,000 ÷ 80,000, or $3.00 per direct labor hour. So that the overhead applied to each job will be obtained by multiplying the labor hours used on the job by $3.00.

Under certain conditions the overhead may be applied in proportion to the direct labor cost. The rate of application is then obtained by dividing the estimated overhead for the year by the estimated direct labor cost. For example, if in the above case it were estimated that the direct cost for the year would be $300,000, then, $240,000 ÷ $300,000 would give an overhead application rate of 80 per cent of direct labor cost.

Sometimes the overhead is applied according to the number of hours the machines have been operated. If the estimated number of machine hours in our illustrative case were 400,000, then $240,000 ÷ 400,000 would give a rate of overhead application of $.60 per machine hour.

In practice the manufacturing overhead is usually called burden.

COST CENTERS

For purposes of cost accounting the factory is divided into cost centers. A cost center may be what is usually referred to as a department: an area where a certain type of work is performed, such as machining, assembling, and finishing; or forming, plating, and polishing. But for various reasons it may consist of an operation by a certain machine. However, for convenience, the cost centers are commonly referred to as departments and will be so called in the following discussion.

DEPARTMENTALIZATION OF OVERHEAD

In some cases it is found more equitable to use a different rate of overhead application for each department of the factory. This requires that the record of indirect costs be kept by departments and an estimate for each department made at the beginning of the year to determine the rate to be used for the application of the departmental overhead of each job.

In addition to the cost centers engaged in turning out the products, or *production departments*, a factory has various *service departments* which render service to the production departments. Among them are such departments as the power plant, plant manager's office, building service (including depreciation, insurance, property taxes, and so forth), industrial relations, and stores department.

Since the application of overhead cost to production is based on the overhead of the production departments, the cost of the service departments must first be distributed in some reasonable manner to the production departments to which they render service. This may be done, for example, as follows:

Department	Distribution Basis
Power plant	Floor space occupied
Plant manager's office	Direct labor cost
Building service	Floor space occupied
Industrial relations	Number of employees in department
Stores	Number of requisitions filled

After having distributed the service department costs to production departments, all indirect costs will be classified according to production departments. Not only may different rates be used for the application of overhead of the various departments to production but also different methods, such as direct labor hours, direct labor cost, or machine hours. The procedure to be used will be determined by whoever is in charge of production.

JOB COST SHEET

JOB NO. 1877
UNITS 1,000

DESCRIPTION 3" Electires

MATERIAL				LABOR				OVERHEAD				
DATE	REQ. NO.	DEPT.	AMOUNT	DATE	DEPT.	HRS.	AMOUNT	DATE	MACH. HRS.	DEPT.	RATE	AMOUNT
1964 May 4	1826	1	875.20	1964 May 8	1	47	105.75	May 8		1	2.60	122.20
12	1908	2	137.85	15	2	22	49.50	15	20	2	.60	12.00
20	1937	3	26.50	22	3	8	18.00	22		3	80%	14.40
			1,039.55				173.25					148.60

SUMMARY

MATERIAL	1,039.55
LABOR	173.25
OVERHEAD	148.60
TOTAL COST	1,361.40
UNIT COST	1.3614

168

JOB COST SHEET

A job cost sheet is illustrated on page 168. It is the record of the cost of a job and constitutes a statement which the executive will refer to for this information.

Job No. 1872 calls for 1,000, 3″ electites. The factory has three departments, Nos. 1, 2, and 3. In Department 1 the overhead is applied at the rate of $2.60 per labor hour, in Department 2 at the rate of $.60 per machine hour, and in Department 3 at the rate of 80 per cent of direct labor cost. Since the cost of the job is $1,361.40, the unit cost per electite is $1.3614.

When a job has been completed the cost sheet for that job is removed from the record of work in process and filed. Some jobs are for stock while others are to be shipped immediately to customers. The goods manufactured for stock are placed in the stockroom and recorded in the finished goods inventory; the cost of those shipped to customers is recorded in the record of cost of goods sold.

The total of all costs recorded on the cost sheets of unfinished jobs constitutes the inventory of work in process.

FLOW OF COSTS

During the month of May, 1964, the factory processed four jobs, three of which were completed: Nos. 1872 and 1873 for stock, and 1874 for immediate shipment. Job No. 1875 remained unfinished. There was no work in process at the beginning of the month.

The flow of costs is illustrated in the following diagram:

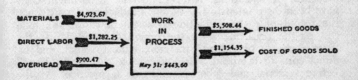

PRODUCTION STATEMENT
MONTH OF MAY, 1964

Job No.	Material	Labor	Overhead	Total
1872	$1,039.55	$ 173.25	$148.60	$1,361.40
1873	2,725.62	895.00	526.42	4,147.04
To finished
stock	$3,765.17	$1,068.25	$675.02	$5,508.44
1874	$ 895.00	$ 126.50	$132.85	$1,154.35
To cost of
goods sold ...	$ 895.00	$ 126.50	$132.85	$1,154.35
Total finished
production ..	$4,660.17	$1,194.75	$807.87	$6,662.79
1875
(In process) ..	$ 263.50	$ 87.50	$ 92.60	$ 443.60
Total costs	$4,923.67	$1,282.25	$900.47	$7,106.39

PRODUCTION STATEMENT

At the end of each month there is prepared a production statement which summarizes the costs of all jobs processed during the month and indicates their disposition. Such a statement for our illustrative case is shown above.

Process Cost Accounting

In process cost accounting, as stated above, the costs are accumulated by cost centers, that is, stages in production, or processes, or operations. After the service department costs have been distributed to the various production departments, the record of each production department shows the total cost of the department for the period subdivided into the three elements of (direct) material, (direct) labor, and indirect costs or overhead. For convenience the word "direct" before material and labor is omitted in practice. As the period used is almost invariably a month, this unit of time will be assumed in the following discussion.

INDIRECT COSTS

It was seen that in job order cost accounting a conventional procedure is used to apportion the manufacturing overhead, or burden, to the jobs. Since under process cost procedure all costs are accumulated according to the departments in which they are incurred, apportionment is usually not necessary. Indirect labor is recorded among the costs of the department in which it is performed, indirect material the department using it, and depreciation the department where the assets depreciated are located. However, in some process systems the indirect costs are first accumulated for the factory as a whole and then apportioned to the departments.

CASE: PROCESSING COMPLETED DAILY

Consider the case of the manufacturer of a food product for which production is started and finished each day. Three stages are required in production, called processes K, L, and M. The factory has two service departments, R and S.

During the month of June, 1964, the indirect costs were:

Production Departments

Department K	$3,625
Department L	1,721
Department M	2,405

Service Departments

Department R	852
Department S	1,233

The costs of the service departments are divided one third to each of the production departments, making the total of the overhead of the production departments:

Department K	$4,320
Department L	2,416
Department M	3,100

The production for the month was 2,000 units. It is summarized in the production statement on page 173.

WORK IN PROCESS

In job order cost accounting the total of the costs recorded on the cost sheets of unfinished jobs constitutes the inventory of work in process. This inventory is thus easily obtained. But in process cost accounting the determination of the inventory of work in process is more difficult.

The total departmental cost for a month must be divided between the finished production and the work in process. For this purpose it is necessary first to obtain the number of units produced and then the cost per unit. The unit cost multiplied by the number of units in process gives the inventory of work in process. But the units in process are partly finished units. Multiplying by partly finished units will not allocate the cost equitably.

In order to allocate cost to the units in process, accountants have adopted another conventional procedure. It is to convert the units in process into *equivalent units* on the basis of an estimate of the extent of completion. To illustrate: if there are 1,000 units in process one-half complete, they are considered the equivalent of 500 completed units.

CASE: WORK CONTINUALLY IN PROCESS

A certain factory has two processes called Process O and Process P. The production statement, giving both costs and quantities, for the month of July, 1964, is found on pages 176–77. Let us see how it was prepared.

The material, labor, and factory overhead costs are obtained from the departmental records. They are listed in the production report to begin with. Note that work was in process in Process P at the beginning of the month and in both processes at the end.

Computation of equivalent units. The first step is to compute the equivalent units produced in each process. In most manufacturing processes labor is performed and factory overhead accumulates at an even rate but materials are commonly not put into process continuously. Materials are most likely

PRODUCTION STATEMENT
MONTH OF JUNE, 1964

COST OF PRODUCTION

	DEPT. K		DEPT. L		DEPT. M		TOTAL	
	AMOUNT	UNIT COST	AMOUNT	UNIT COST	AMOUNT	UNIT COST	AMOUNT	UNIT COST
Material	$18,872	$ 9.436	$ 5,420	$2.710	—	—	$24,292	$12.146
Labor	9,500	4.750	4,320	2.160	$5,274	$2.637	19,094	9.547
Factory overhead	4,320	2.160	2,416	1.208	3,100	1.550	9,836	4.918
Total	$32,692	$16.346	$12,156	$6.078	$8,374	$4.187	$53,222	$26.611

QUANTITY PRODUCED: 2,000 units

173

to be put into process at the beginning of an operation, particularly in the first stage. Sometimes they go in at the end of an operation as, for instance, when the materials used are containers. Therefore, in most cases separate computations of equivalent units are made for materials and for labor and overhead.

The computation of equivalent units produced follows the sequence: units completed, plus final inventory (in equivalent units), minus initial inventory (in equivalent units). This is seen in the schedule of equivalent units produced for the illustrative case which follows.

SCHEDULE OF EQUIVALENT UNITS PRODUCED

MATERIAL

	Process O	Process P
Units completed	4,400	4,300
Final inventory (in equivalent units)	600	500
	5,000	4,800
Less Initial inventory		
(in equivalent units)	—	400
Equivalent units produced	5,000	4,400

LABOR AND OVERHEAD

	Process O	Process P
Units completed	4,400	4,300
Final inventory (in equivalent units)	200	200
	4,600	4,500
Less Initial inventory		
(in equivalent units)	—	200
Equivalent units produced	4,600	4,300

From the quantity section of the production report it is seen that the final inventory of work in process of Process O consisted of 600 units with materials complete, 33⅓ per cent of the labor performed, and 33⅓ per cent of the overhead applied. Therefore, the equivalent units in the inventory are 600 for materials and 200 for labor and overhead.

The initial inventory of Process P consisted of 400 units with materials complete, 50 per cent of the labor performed, and 50 per cent of the overhead applied. Therefore, the equivalent units in the inventory were 400 for materials and 200 for labor and overhead.

The final inventory of Process P consisted of 500 units with materials complete, 40 per cent of the labor performed and 40 per cent of the overhead applied. Therefore, the equivalent units in the inventory were 500 for materials and 200 for labor and overhead.

Computation of unit costs. Having computed the equivalent units, the unit costs are obtained by dividing the material cost of each process by the equivalent units for materials and the labor and overhead costs by the equivalent units for labor and overhead.

Computation of work in process inventory. The inventories of work in process of the two processes, the total of which is the inventory of work in process to the business as of July 31, 1964, are obtained as shown in the schedule of work in process on page 178.

Computation of cost of goods transferred. The total cost of production of Process O for the month is $19,080. Since $1,480 of the cost has been allocated to work in process, the difference is the cost of the goods transferred to Process P, $17,600, with a unit cost of $4.00.

The total cost of production of Process P for the month is $13,225, with a unit cost of $2.75. Adding the transfer from Process O, makes a total of $30,825, with a unit cost of $6.75. Deducting the final inventory of work in process, $3,000, leaves a difference of $27,825, the cost of the goods transferred to the finished goods inventory. This is arrived at as shown in the schedule of cost of finished goods on page 179.

Although the unit cost of production in Process P for the month of July, 1964, is $6.75, when the total cost of goods finished during the month, $27,825, is divided by 4,300 units, it is found that the unit cost is $6.4703. This is caused by the relatively lower costs in the July 1 inventory of work in process in Process P.

It should be noted that the cost of the work in process at the beginning of the month, including the cost in the prior process, is assigned to the finished goods rather than to the work in process. This is done on the first-in, first-out principle for it is reasonable to assume that the goods in process at the beginning of the period were finished first.

PRODUCTION STATEMENT
MONTH OF JULY, 1964

COST OF PRODUCTION

	PROCESS O		PROCESS P		TOTAL	
	COST	PER UNIT	COST	PER UNIT	COST	PER UNIT
Work in process, July 1	$ —	$ —	$ 1,250	$ —	$ 1,250	$ —
Material	8,500	1.70	6,600	1.50	15,100	3.20
Labor	6,900	1.50	4,300	1.00	11,200	2.50
Factory overhead	3,680	.80	1,075	.25	4,755	1.05
Total	$19,080	$4.00	$13,225	$2.75	$32,305	$6.75
Transferred in	—	—	17,600	4.00	—	—
	$19,080	$4.00	$30,825	$6.75	$32,305	$6.75
Less Work in process, July 31	1,480	—	3,000	—	4,480	—
Transferred to Process P	$17,600	$4.00				
Transferred to finished goods			$27,825	$6.75	$27,825	$6.4703

176

QUANTITY OF PRODUCTION (UNITS)

	PROCESS O	PROCESS P
QUANTITY TO BE ACCOUNTED FOR:		
Work in process, July 1		400
Degree of completion:		
Material		(100%)
Labor and overhead		(50%)
		4,400
Put into process or received from preceding department	5,000	
To be accounted for	5,000	4,800
	=====	=====
QUANTITY ACCOUNTED FOR AS FOLLOWS:		
Transferred to next department or to finished goods	4,400	4,300
Work in process, July 31	600	500
Degree of completion:		
Material	(100%)	(100%)
Labor and overhead	(33⅓%)	(40%)
Total accounted for	5,000	4,800
	=====	=====

SCHEDULE OF WORK IN PROCESS
JULY 31, 1964

Process O

MATERIAL

 600 units @ $1.70 .... $1,020

LABOR

 200 equivalent units @ $1.50 300

OVERHEAD

 200 equivalent units @ $.80 160

     Work in process $1,480

Process P

PRIOR PROCESS COSTS

 500 units @ $4.00 .... $2,000

MATERIAL

 500 units @ $1.50 750

LABOR

 200 equivalent units @ $1.00 200

OVERHEAD

 200 equivalent units @ $.25 50

     Work in process $3,000

COMPLEX SITUATIONS

The foregoing is a very simple case. In practice such processes are found as:

Sequential processing. There are several products but all are processed through the same departmental sequence.

Parallel processing. Different products follow similar sequences but in different departments. For example, product

SCHEDULE OF COST OF FINISHED GOODS
MONTH OF JULY, 1964

TRANSFERRED OUT OF PROCESS P: 4,300 units

FROM INITIAL INVENTORY: 400 units

Balance, July 1		$ 1,250
Added in Process P:		
Labor, 200 equivalent		
units @ $1.00	$200	
Overhead, 200 equivalent		
units @ $.25	50	250
		$ 1,500

STARTED THIS PERIOD: 3,900 units

3,900 units @ $6.75	26,325
Cost of 4,300 units finished ..	$27,825

A might be processed in Departments 1, 2, and 3, and product B in Departments 4, 5, and 6.

Selective processing. The various products follow different sequences. For example, product C might be processed in Departments 1 and 3, product D in Departments 3 and 5, product E in Departments 2 and 5, and product F in Departments 2 and 4. Also, in some cases, all products might be finished in a Department 6.

Additional complications are encountered when, as in some industries, there is normal spoilage or loss, while, common to all, there may be abnormal spoilage. For their treatment the reader is referred to specialized books on cost accounting.

Joint-Product Costs

Joint products are two or more products that are automatically produced together. They cannot be produced separately. The production of meat inevitably produces hides, shortening, hair, fertilizer, and other products. Petroleum refining produces gasoline, kerosene, naphtha, and fuel oil. Flour milling produces not only several grades of flour but also bran and wheat germ.

The joint products are processed together to a point of

separation at which some are ready for sale while others require further processing. The *joint costs* are those incurred in processing the joint products up to the point of separation or *split-off point*. Joint costs should not be confused with common costs which are those incurred in producing, with the same facilities, two or more products that could be produced separately.

ALLOCATION OF JOINT COSTS

The problem in the matter of joint costs is the allocation of the joint costs to the various products up to the split-off point. This allocation is necessary for inventory pricing. There are two possible methods of allocation: (1) according to physical measures, and (2) according to the relative sales value of the products.

The allocation by physical measurement of the products is in such terms as pounds, gallons, or tons. This method, which assigns the average cost to each unit produced, is usually unacceptable, primarily because it regards the different products as having similar importance. It assumes, for example, that in meat packing the same cost is incurred per pound for beefsteaks, hides, and bones; and in the dairy industry that the same cost is incurred to obtain a gallon of cream as a gallon of skim milk. The effect of such inventory treatment would result in showing a constant loss on the sale of a product that has a low sales price. The inventory is, therefore, usually prepared by allocating cost to the products in proportion to their market value.

FIRST ILLUSTRATIVE CASE

A certain manufacturer produces three products, X, Y, and Z. The joint costs of production for a certain month are:

Material	$240,000
Labor	160,000
Overhead	80,000
Total	$480,000

The units produced, the sales price per unit, and the resulting revenue are:

	Units		Selling Price Per Unit		Revenue
X	70,000	×	$10.00	=	$700,000
Y	20,000	×	4.50	=	90,000
Z	10,000	×	1.00	=	10,000
Total	100,000				$800,000

Dividing the cost of production by the total revenue gives the percentage of cost:

$$\$480,000 \div \$800,000 = 60\%$$

The allocated cost per unit will be:

X	$10.00	×	.60	=	$6.00
Y	4.50	×	.60	=	2.70
Z	1.00	×	.60	=	.60

The total cost of production will be allocated:

X	70,000	×	$6.00	=	$420,000
Y	20,000	×	2.70	=	54,000
Z	10,000	×	.60	=	6,000
		Total			$480,000

By this method the percentage of gross profit is the same for all products,—in this case 40 per cent. Recognition is thus given to the fact that the joint products are the result of the same operation.

Although the method of allocating cost according to market value is preferable to the physical measure method, it is still arbitrary and care should be exercised in making managerial decisions based on this cost allocation.

SECOND ILLUSTRATIVE CASE

Where it is not possible to obtain market quotations for the joint products at the split-off point because they cannot be sold without further processing, the relative inventory values may be calculated by starting with the sales price after further processing and from this deducting the cost to complete in order to arrive at the value before completion which is used as the basis for calculation. This is illustrated by the following case.

A manufacturer produces three commodities, R, S, and T. The following information is available:

	Unit Sales Price	Unit Cost To Complete	Units Produced
R	$55.00	$15.00	2,000
S	30.00	5.00	1,000
T	23.00	3.00	500

Calculations based on the foregoing:

	Unit Value Before Completion		Units Produced		Total Assigned Value Before Completion
R	$40.00	×	2,000	=	$ 80,000
S	25.00	×	1,000	=	25,000
T	20.00	×	500	=	10,000
			Total		$115,000

The cost at the split-off point is $46,000. Therefore:

$$\$46,000 \div \$115,000 = .40\%$$

The allocation of the joint cost is:

R	$80,000	×	.40	=	$32,000
S	25,000	×	.40	=	10,000
T	10,000	×	.40	=	4,000
			Total		$46,000

By-Product Costs

When a joint product is of minor importance it is called a *by-product* and the products of major importance may be called *co-products*. There is no definite basis on which the distinction between a major product and a by-product is made. The distinction depends on what product is sought. In copper mining gold will be a by-product, while in gold mining copper will be a by-product.

The cost of a by-product is given treatment different from that given to the co-products because the sums involved do not justify the same treatment. Depending on the type of operations, by-product values may be given recognition either at the split-off point, on the basis of the market price, estimated price, or sales price less completion cost, or at the time the by-products are sold. The revenue derived from the sale of the by-product may be deducted from the joint costs or may be treated as a separate form of revenue.

14. Manufacturing Costs: Predetermined

THE MOST EFFECTIVE type of cost accounting is that which makes use of predetermined or *standard costs*. This procedure consists of determining, in advance of production, what the unit cost *should be* and, upon completion of production, comparing the actual costs with the standard costs.

SETTING THE STANDARD

In Chapter 13 it was explained that a predetermined rate is established for the allocation of overhead by means of a budget. In standard cost accounting not only is the factory overhead budgeted but also the materials and labor. This is not only done for the factory as a whole but also for a unit of product. There is prepared for each commodity a *standard cost card* which lists the specifications of the materials to be used and the quantity and cost of each, the labor time and rate for each operation in each department, and the amount of factory overhead in each department. It concludes with the unit cost of production.

COST VARIANCES

In standard cost procedure the actual costs of material, labor, and overhead of the work in process are, in general, recorded as in historical cost accounting. But when the work comes out of process and goes into the finished stage it is priced at the standard cost figure. The differences or *variances* between the actual and standard costs are then indicated in the accounting records. This procedure is illustrated in the diagram below.

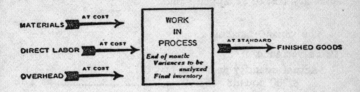

Having ascertained the variances, they are analyzed. Analysis may reveal that either the standard was incorrect or that the actual cost deviated either favorably or unfavorably from the standard. If the variance is found to be unfavorable, the analysis will be conducted further to determine the cause and to fix responsibility therefor. Steps can then be taken to correct the situation. Standard costing is thus an important tool for the control of manufacturing costs.

MATERIALS VARIANCES

There are two materials variances: (1) price, and (2) quantity. The materials price variance is the difference between the price paid and the standard price. The materials quantity variance is the difference between the quantity of material used and the standard quantity of material.

The formulas for the materials variances are:

Price variance = (Actual quantities × Actual prices) − (Actual quantities × Standard prices)
Quantity variance = (Actual quantity × Standard prices − (Standard quantity × Standard prices)

ILLUSTRATIVE CASE

The following facts concerning the use of material are obtained from certain production records:

Price variance, $320
Quantity variance, $300

The standard cost card shows 3,000 pounds of material at $1.50 per pound. Actually, 3,200 pounds of material were used at a cost of $1.60 per pound.

The variance analysis is:

Price variance

Actual quantity at actual price
  3,200 pounds × $1.60 .... $5,120
Actual quantity at standard price
  3,200 pounds × $1.50 4,800
            Variance (unfavorable) .... $ 320

Quantity variance

Actual quantity at standard price
  3,200 pounds × $1.50 .... $4,800
Standard quantity at standard price
  3,000 pounds × $1.50 4,500
            Variance (unfavorable) .... $ 300

This is the accounting analysis. It indicates that more material was used and that a higher price was paid for the material than was specified in the standard. These unfavorable variances require further investigation. However, this is an engineering analysis and so is beyond the scope of the present book. But the reader will readily observe how standard cost accounting procedure aids management by indicating the direction to be pursued by further analysis.

LABOR VARIANCES

There are two labor variances: (1) rate, and (2) time or efficiency. The rate variance is the difference between the actual and the standard cost. The time variance is the difference between the actual and the standard hours at the standard rate.

The formulas for the labor variances are:

Rate variance = (Actual hours × Actual rate) − (Actual hours × Standard rate)

Time variance = (Actual hours × Standard rate) − (Standard hours × Standard rate)

ILLUSTRATIVE CASE

The following facts concerning labor are obtained from certain production records:

Rate variance, $45
Time variance, $125

The standard cost card specifies 400 hours of direct labor at a cost of $2.50 per hour. Actually, 450 hours of direct labor were used at a cost of $2.60 per hour.

The variance analysis is:

Rate variance

Actual hours at actual rate	
450 hours × $2.60	$1,170
Actual hours at standard rate	
450 hours × $2.50	1,125
Variance (unfavorable)	$ 45

Time variance

Actual hours at standard rate	
450 hours × $2.50	$1,125
Standard hours at standard rate	
400 hours × $2.50	1,000
Variance (unfavorable)	$ 125

As in the case of materials, the unfavorable variances in labor cost should be investigated. It should be ascertained why a higher rate was paid and why more hours were worked than specified in the standard cost card.

OVERHEAD STANDARDS

Because of the nature of the manufacturing overhead, the overhead standards are more difficult to set than those for material and labor. The material and labor costs are closely related to the articles manufactured. But much of the overhead is not directly related to production. In fact, some of the overhead costs, such as superintendence and rent, depreciation, taxes, and insurance on the factory building are usually not only not directly related to production but would continue if production were suspended. Such overhead costs are known as *fixed costs*.

On the other hand, certain overhead costs vary directly with production. Among these are light and power, repairs and repair parts, and certain indirect labor. Such costs that vary with the volume of production are called *variable costs*.

Then there are certain overhead costs that are not definitely fixed nor do they vary directly in proportion to production, such as inspection and payroll taxes. These are known as *semivariable costs*.

It is accordingly seen that the problem of setting overhead cost standards involves taking into consideration the effect of the changes in the overhead as the volume of production increases. In order to do this there is prepared a *flexible budget* in which the factory overhead is estimated for different production levels, usually as percentages of capacity. In this budget the fixed and variable overhead are shown separately, the semivariable portion usually being divided in some reasonable manner between the fixed and the variable. So that, for example, in a certain factory at 80 per cent of capacity the budgeted overhead might be: fixed, $250,000, variable, $200,000; and at 90 per cent of capacity it might be: fixed, $250,000, variable, $225,000, and so forth.

OVERHEAD VARIANCES

There are three manufacturing overhead variances: (1) spending, (2) capacity, and (3) time or efficiency. The spending variance is the difference between the actual overhead cost and the standard cost specified in the budget. The capacity variance is the difference between the number of hours worked and the standard specified in the budget. The time variance is the difference between the number of hours worked and the standard for the product.

The formulas for the overhead variances are:

Spending variance = (Actual overhead cost) − (Budgeted overhead cost for the actual production hours)

Capacity variance = (Budgeted overhead cost for the actual production hours) − (Actual hours × Standard rate)

Time variance = (Actual hours × Standard rate) − (Standard hours for operations completed × Standard rate)

ILLUSTRATIVE CASE

The budget of a certain factory shows:

	Per Cent of Capacity	
	90%	100%
Standard hours	18,000	20,000
Fixed expense	$8,000	$ 8,000
Variable expense	9,000	10,000

The standard volume was estimated at 100 per cent of capacity, or 20,000 standard hours. Therefore, the standard expense rate was:

Fixed: $ 8,000 ÷ 20,000 = $.40
Variable: 10,000 ÷ 20,000 = .50
          Total .... $.90

The production records show:

Production at 90 per cent of capacity:
Standard hours for actual production 18,000
Actual hours used 18,400
Actual expense
   Fixed .... $ 8,000
   Variable 10,200
                   Total actual expense $18,200

The records showed the following variances:

                   Spending variance, $1,000
                   Capacity variance, $640
                   Time variance, $360

The variance analysis is:

Spending variance·
   Actual expense $18,200
   Budget adjusted to 18,400 actual hours
      Variable expense: 18,400 × $.50 ...... $9,200
      Fixed expense 8,000   17,200
                   Variance (unfavorable) .... $ 1,000

Capacity variance
    Budget adjusted to 18,400 actual hours $17,200
    Actual hours × standard rate
        18,400 × \$.90 16,560
                Variance (unfavorable) .... $ 640

Time variance
    Actual hours × standard rate $16,560
    Standard hours for operations completed ×
        standard rate 18,000 × \$.90 16,200
                Variance (unfavorable) .... $ 360

The accountant's analysis reveals that the overhead cost exceeded the standard by \$1,000, that because of not meeting the budgeted use of capacity, or idle time, there was an unfavorable variance of \$640, and that because 400 hours were used in excess of the number of hours called for in the budget for the actual production there was an unfavorable variance of \$360. The investigation to be pursued by the management is thus indicated.

15. Cost—Volume—Profit Analysis

THE PROBLEMS in connection with the control of operations tend to cluster about the relationship of cost, volume, and profit. For the analysis of this relationship, use is made of the separation of fixed costs and variable costs. As explained in Chapter 14, costs may be divided into three categories: (1) *fixed costs*, those that are not affected by the degree of business activity (2) *variable costs*, those that vary with activity, and (3) *semivariable costs*, those that vary but not directly with the degree of activity.

For the purpose of analysis based on the cost-volume-profit relationship, a twofold classification is used: (1) fixed costs, and (2) variable costs. The fixed element of the semivariable costs is included among the fixed costs and the variable element among the variable costs. For example, take the case of salaries. A business requires a certain minimum staff regardless of the sales volume, the salaries of which are a fixed cost. As sales increase, more help will be required; their salaries are a variable cost. The separation of the fixed and variable components of the semivariable costs requires judgment.

MARGINAL INCOME STATEMENT

The traditional income statement does not classify the expenses as required for the cost-volume-profit analysis. It must, accordingly, be recast for this purpose. Note that the word *expenses* has been used instead of *costs*. Since expenses are expired costs, the income statement, which is historical in nature, reports on expired costs or expenses. The revised

income statement is called the *marginal income statement*.
It follows the sequence:

Sales (net) – Variable expenses = Marginal income
Marginal income – Fixed expenses = Net income

Marginal income, also known as *contribution income*, is
the contribution to fixed expense and net income. In the
case of corporations, use of net income before federal income
taxes is preferred because the taxes vary approximately with
net income before taxes.

ILLUSTRATION OF PROFIT PLANNING

The following is the income statement of a merchandising
business in traditional form:

JOHN DAVIS
INCOME STATEMENT
FOR YEAR ENDED DECEMBER 31, 1963

Sales (net)		$240,000
Cost of goods sold		130,000
Gross margin		$110,000
Selling expenses	$48,000	
Administrative expenses	12,000	60,000
Net income for the year		$ 50,000

Having analyzed the expenses into the categories of variable expenses and fixed expenses, the statement is recast as
follows:

JOHN DAVIS
MARGINAL INCOME STATEMENT
For Year Ended December 31, 1963

Sales (net) $240,000

Less—Variable expenses:

     Cost of goods sold $130,000

     Selling expenses 40,000

     Administrative expenses 10,000

       Total variable expenses 180,000*

       Marginal income .... $ 60,000

Less—Fixed expenses:

     Selling expenses $8,000

     Administrative expenses 2,000

       Total fixed expenses 10,000

       Net income for the year .... $ 50,000

*75% of net sales

Using this statement as a basis, a study of the relationship of cost, volume, and profit may be made.

BREAK-EVEN POINT

In every business there is a certain sales volume at which the business will have neither a profit nor a loss. This is known as the *break-even point*. Until this volume is reached the business will operate at a loss and after it has been reached the business will operate at a profit. It is obviously important for the management to know where this point lies.

To illustrate: if the income statement of a certain business is as follows the business is said to break even.

Sales (net)	$15,000

Less—Expenses:

Fixed	$ 4,000
Variable	11,000
Total expenses	15,000
Net income for the year	$ 0

From this the following formula for the break-even point is derived:

(1) Sales   =   Fixed expenses + Variable expenses; or
     $15,000 = $4,000   + $11,000
(2) Sales −Variable expenses =   Fixed expenses
     $15,000 − $11,000   = $4,000

Applying the second form of the formula to the case of John Davis and using the letter S for sales at the break-even point, we have (since the variable expenses, $180,000, are 75 per cent of the sales):

$$S - .75S = \$10,000$$
Deducting 75 per cent of S from total S gives
$$.25S = \$10,000$$
And if 25 per cent of S = $10,000, then
$$S = \$40,000$$

The sales must amount to $40,000 for the business to break even. Assuming that the commodities sold, called the *sales mix*, are priced at an average of $8.00 each, 5,000 units will have to be sold. These facts can be shown graphically on what is called a *break-even chart*, as seen on page 196.

The chart can be extended to show what the net income will be for any given sales volume. Note that when 10,000 units are sold for $80,000 the net income will be $10,000. Here is a neat diagram on which management can see the results for any sales volume.

However, this neat diagram does not give the precise information it appears to give. This is so because the reclassification of the semivariable costs, although it may be done with great care, cannot be done with precision. This, however, does not detract from the usefulness of the break-even analysis as long as its conclusions are regarded as approximations.

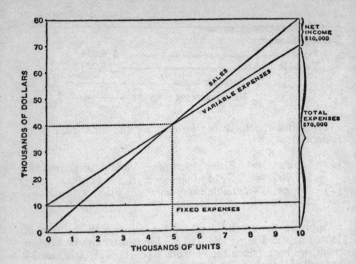

ILLUSTRATION OF DECISION MAKING

A certain business is considering an expansion of facilities. The income statement for the past year is:

Sales (net)		$350,000
Less—Expenses:		
Fixed	$ 75,000	
Variable	140,000	
Total expenses		215,000
Net income for the year		$135,000

The break-even calculation is:

$$S = \$ 75,000 + .40S$$
$$S - .40S = \$ 75,000$$
$$.60S = \$ 75,000$$
$$S = \$125,000$$

It is estimated that the increase in facilities will increase fixed expenses by $15,000 annually, mainly on account of depreciation. Under the proposed conditions the break-even point calculation is:

$$S = \$\ 90,000 + .40S$$
$$S - .40S = \$\ 90,000$$
$$.60S = \$\ 90,000$$
$$S = \$150,000$$

The break-even point will under proposed conditions be raised by $25,000. Therefore, sales will have to be increased to this extent in order to break even. They will also have to be increased by $25,000 to maintain present earnings, as shown by the following calculation:

Let S' = the sales required to maintain present earnings. Then

$$S' = \$\ 90,000 + .40S' + \$135,000$$

$$\text{(present earnings)}$$
$$S' - .40S' = \$225,000$$
$$.60S' = \$225,000$$
$$S' = \$375,000$$

Proof:

Present sales $350,000
Add sales necessary
    to maintain present earnings   25,000
                                                      $375,000

If the management believes that after the expansion has taken place it will be able to increase sales by at least $25,000 it may proceed with the plans to expand its facilities.

Comparison may also be made of the profit limits under present and proposed conditions. If the maximum sales capacity with present facilities is $400,000 and under proposed conditions it would be $500,000, the following comparison may be made:

	Under Present Conditions	Under Proposed Conditions
Sales (net)	$400,000	$500,000
Less—Fixed expenses	75,000	90,000
	$325,000	$410,000
Less—Variable expenses		
(40% of sales)	160,000	200,000
Profit limits	$165,000	$210,000

From this it is seen that when operating at full capacity under proposed conditions the earnings will be $45,000 greater than under present conditions.

It has been assumed in the above computation that the proportion of variable expenses to sales will remain unchanged. If not, the variable expense figure will have to be properly adjusted.

DIRECT COSTING

The cost-volume-profit analysis is incorporated into cost accounting by means of a technique known as *direct costing*. This may be used in a job order or process system with either historical or standard costing procedure.

In direct costing the direct material and direct labor are treated in the manner described in Chapters 13 and 14. However, in accounting for the manufacturing overhead the variable costs are separated from the fixed costs. The variable costs are designated as *product costs* because they are considered as having been incurred for specific amounts of production. The fixed costs are not considered as costs of production but rather as costs of being ready to produce and so are designated as *period costs* and treated as expenses of the accounting period. Because the variable overhead costs are applied directly to production, the procedure has been given the name of direct costing in contrast to the traditional procedure which is then referred to as *absorption costing* since all costs are absorbed into the cost of goods manufactured.

An income statement prepared under the direct costing procedure is shown on page 200.

DIRECT VERSUS ABSORPTION COSTING

Since under traditional or absorption costing the fixed as well as the variable overhead is absorbed into the cost of goods manufactured, when relatively fewer units are produced the fixed overhead will be greater per unit. This results in a higher unit cost of production carried into the finished goods inventory. It sometimes happens that a considerable portion of such goods with a high unit cost is carried into the next period, thus causing the cost of goods sold for the period to be relatively high. If in this period there should be a large volume of sales, the income statement for the period might well show a decline in net income in spite of the high sales activity. This seeming inconsistency often puzzles the non-accounting executive.

Direct costing overcomes this confusing phenomenon by supplying management with the *marginal income* figure as a substitute for the *gross margin* used under absorption costing, thus eliminating the effect of the fixed manufacturing overhead on production costs. The marginal income figure is more sensitive to the effects of production efficiency than the gross margin figure and is a better guide for managerial control.

A disadvantage in direct costing is that its treatment of the fixed overhead conflicts with accepted accounting principles in two respects: (1) the final inventory of finished goods is understated because it does not contain the fixed manufacturing overhead, and (2) the net income is understated because the fixed overhead that under generally accepted procedure would be included in the inventory and deferred is deducted from revenue. Probably for this reason direct costing has not been widely accepted. However, some companies use the direct costing figures internally for managerial purposes and adjust them to the traditional basis for external reporting.

OPERATIONS PLANNING

In planning operations, studies may be made of the effects of changes in the cost-volume-profit relationship.

Sales (net)		$150,000
Less—Cost of goods sold:		
Direct materials	$19,250	
Direct labor	16,800	
Variable manufacturing overhead	14,750	
Total variable production costs	$50,800	
Add—Initial inventory of work in process	5,600	
	$56,400	
Less—Final inventory of work in process	6,500	
Cost of goods manufactured	$49,900	
Add—Initial inventory of finished goods	17,200	
	$67,100	
Less—Final inventory of finished goods	18,500	
Production cost of goods sold	$48,600	
Add—Variable selling expenses	17,500	
Variable administrative expenses	5,000	
Total cost of goods sold		71,100
Marginal income		$ 78,900
Less—Fixed expenses:		
Factory overhead	$10,800	
Selling expenses	8,500	
Administrative expenses	5,000	
Total fixed expenses		24,300
Operating income		$ 54,600

Given the following budget:

		% of Sales
Sales (net)	$153,000	100.0%
Variable expenses	112,000	73.2
Marginal income	$ 41,000	26.8%
Fixed expenses	13,000	
Operating income	$ 28,000	

Using the formula for the sales at the break-even point derived earlier in this chapter, the following is obtained:

$$S - .732S = \$13,000$$
$$.268S = \$13,000$$
$$S = \$48,507$$

Note that the result is the same as would be obtained by dividing the fixed expenses by the percentage of marginal income to sales.

Increase in fixed expenses. Assuming a 5 per cent increase in fixed expenses, the budget would be:

		% of Sales
Sales (net)	$153,000	100.0%
Variable expenses	112,000	73.2
Marginal income	$ 41,000	26.8%
Fixed expenses		
(105% of $13,000)	13,650	
Operating income	$ 27,350	

The sales at the break-even point would be:

$$.268S = \$13,650$$
$$S = \$50,933$$

The marginal income would not change but the operating income would be reduced by $650 and the break-even point raised by $2,426.

Increase in variable expenses. Assuming an increase of 5 per cent in variable expenses, the budget would be:

		% of Sales
Sales (net)	$153,000	100.0%
Variable expenses		
(105% of $112,000)	117,600	76.9
Marginal income...............	$ 35,400	23.1%
Fixed expenses	13,000	
Operating income...............	$ 22,400	

The sales at the break-even point would be:

$$.231S = \$13,000$$
$$S = \$56,277$$

The break-even point would be raised by $7,770, the marginal income decreased to 23.1%, and the operating income decreased by $5,600.

Increase in selling prices. Assuming a 5 per cent increase in selling prices, the budget would be:

		% of Sales
Sales (net) (105% of $153,000)	$160,650	100.0%
Variable expenses	112,000	69.7
Marginal income...............	$ 48,650	30.3%
Fixed expenses	13,000	
Operating income...............	$ 35,650	

The break-even point would be:

$$.303S = \$13,000$$
$$S = \$42,904$$

The break-even point would be lowered by $5,603, the marginal income increased to 30.3 per cent, and the operating income increased by $7,650.

In the above calculations it was assumed that there would be no change in the product mix. Any important change would have a material effect and, therefore, the budget would have to be revised to take it into consideration.

Index

Recommended MENTOR Books

(0451)

☐ **THE AFFLUENT SOCIETY by John Kenneth Galbraith.** Third Revised Edition. The book that added a new phrase to our language, a new classic to literature, and changed the basic economic attitudes of our age. In this new revision, Galbraith has extensively updated the information and widened the perspectives of his basic argument "... Daring ... a compelling challenge to conventional thought."—*The New York Times*
(621867—$3.95)

☐ **THE NEW INDUSTRIAL STATE by John Kenneth Galbraith.** Third Revised Edition. One of our most distinguished economists and author of such bestsellers as *The Affluent Society* offers a comprehensive look at modern economic life and the changes that are shaping its future.
(620291—$3.95)

☐ **UNDERSTANDING THE ECONOMY: For People Who Can't Stand Economics by Alfred L. Malabre, Jr.** The U.S. economic scene made easily comprehensible and intensely interesting ... "Millions of readers can learn from this lively book."—Paul Samuelson, Nobel Prize-winning economist.
(621409—$3.50)

☐ **BAD MONEY by L.J. Davis.** "The author has managed to integrate such seemingly disparate events of the 1970s as the collapse of the railroads in the Northeast; the bankruptcy of a major mass retailer; the overextension of some of our largest banks; the OPEC connection; the Eurodollar economy; and the attempt to corner the silver markets. All of these point to the dangers which should be of enormous concern ..."—Senator Frank Church
(622456—$3.50)*

*Price is $3.95 in Canada

**Buy them at your local
bookstore or use coupon
on next page for ordering.**

Titles of Related Interest from MENTOR and SIGNET